Railway Memories No.

CHESTERFIELD, STAVELEY & THE HOPE VALLEY

Stephen Chapman

"...so we left the Peak, and went to Chesterfield......a handsome, populous town, well built and well inhabited..."
Daniel Defoe

BELLCODE BOOKS
Church View, Middle Street
Rudston, East Yorkshire YO25 4UF
email: bellcode4books@yahoo.co.uk

ISBN 9781871233 33 9

Designed and edited by Stephen Chapman

Printed in the UK by the Amadeus Press, Cleckheaton, West Yorkshire.

ABOVE: Staveley is well remembered for its great iron works and its internal railway system of mesmerising complexity. Also well remembered are the engines supplied by British Railways' Barrow Hill shed to assist the works' own shunters under an agreement going back to early Midland Railway days. The "Staveley tanks" as they were often referred to, included the Johnson 1F 0-6-0s, such as No. 41804 pictured here hard at work somewhere within the works' tangle of lines. *Tom Greaves*
FRONT COVER: Everyday life on the railways around Chesterfield in days gone by. Class 04/5 2-8-0 No. 63726 approaches Heath on the Great Central main line with an Annesley-bound coal train after the 1 in 100 slog up the bank from Staveley. On the right are the sidings for the Williamthorpe Colliery branch while the tracks on the far left are for the station goods yard. *P.J.Hughes/Colour-Rail*
BACK COVER TOP: The roofless roundhouse at Hasland motive power depot in 1963 with a varied selection of locomotives present. The long elevated siding in the background is the shunting neck for Avenue coking plant. *T.B.Owen/Colour-Rail*
BACK COVER BOTTOM: Johnson 1F tank No. 41708 in her natural iron works setting and who would think this wasn't Staveley Works. Doing a faultless impression of her Staveley shunting days, she is seen at Workington steel works on Thursday 12th September 2002. *Stephen Chapman*
FRONTISPIECE: A scene that is unmistakenly Chesterfield Midland way back in LMS days. The twisted spire of St. Mary And All Saints Church climbs above the veteran coach as Hughes-Fowler "Crab" 2-6-0 No. 13056 prepares to leave with a Sheffield-bound express bearing reporting tablet No. 9. *Stephen Chapman archive*

The publisher's thanks are due to all those who have provided material for this edition of Railway Memories, especially Robert Anderson, Adrian Booth, Tom Greaves and Ron Hollier for their additional help. **Sources:** BR, LNER and LMS documents, working timetables, appendices, notices, press releases and publicity publications; Chesterfield Museum; Clinker's Register of Closed Lines and Stations; Durham Mining Museum; Industrial Railway Society; LNER List of Lines; The Midland Through the Peak, Brian Radford, Unicorn Books; The Railway Clearing House Official Handbook of Stations 1938 and 1956; The Ordnance Survey; A Regional History of Railways, The East Midlands by Robin Leleux, David & Charles; the Study Library.net; contempory editions of Modern Railways, Railway Magazine, The Railway Observer, Railway World and Trains Illustrated. ***Bellcode Books is not in a position to supply or locate copies of photographs reproduced in this book. Photographs and downloads can be purchased online or on ebay from some of the agencies credited in the picture captions.***

INTRODUCTION

Inside Chesterfield's Saint Mary and All Saints church, famed for its twisted spire, there is a tomb which firmly proclaims the town's prominence at the dawn of a great industry which spread around the globe and which remains as important to everyday life as ever. It is the resting place of George Stephenson, who engineered the first main line railway, made the train a commercially viable form of transport and built Chesterfield's first railway - one of the country's earliest long-distance trunk main lines. He also founded the great Clay Cross Coal & Iron Company and upon retirement in 1838 went to live at Tapton House, and so he still resides in Chesterfield to this day.

From early beginnings iron, coal and steam combined to establish Chesterfield as the metropolis for a cluster of iron works, collieries and engineering plants knitted together by an entanglement of railways built to serve their needs. And as any regular traveller on the Midland line south of Sheffield will notice, all principal services call at Chesterfield's surviving station - there were once three - be they bound for London, the Midlands, the West Country or Scotland. It has always been a busy focal point for freight traffic using the Rother Valley(the "Old Road") and Hope Valley lines and remains a popular location for railway observers and photographers.

But this book is about more than Chesterfield. It also features the scenic Hope Valley line to Chinley, the much-missed Great Central main line, and the lesser railways east of the town built to serve the many collieries and coke works that once provided local wealth and employment.

On 7th September 1964, British Railways began using the 24-hour clock in its working timetables so we use am/pm up to that date and the 24-hour clock thereafter. Likewise 1961 when train classification changed from an alphabetical system to a four-character reporting number. BR Sectional Appendix supplements are quoted herein as the date for various changes to signalling etc. It should be noted that the actual change may have taken place before the supplement was issued.

Contents

The Hope Valley line has provided a valuable link across the Pennines and no less so today. In this early 1960s scene, 4F 0-6-0 No. 44574 slogs westward with a class 6 partly fitted express freight. The train has just passed Bamford and on the left is the site of sidings which around 50 years earlier connected with a seven-mile light railway that climbed 500ft in order to supply materials for the construction of Derwent, Howden, and again between 1935 and 1946 Ladybower, reservoirs at 1000ft above sea level. *Tom Greaves*

A STORY OF RAILS, COAL AND IRON

AS Chesterfield's Anglo-Saxon name indicates, the first English farmers migrating from continental Europe during the Dark Ages found the remains of a Roman fort with commanding views across open countryside. To the west, the distant wild heights of the Peak District rich in lead and other minerals; in nearby hills coal and iron were near the surface. The market, dating from the 13th century, became a trading point for these commodities and so, during the course of the Industrial Revolution, Chesterfield would find itself surrounded by mining, iron working and heavy engineering while retaining a certain olde worlde charm to this day. In his *A Tour Through the Whole Island of Great Britain 1724-27,* pamphletist and author Daniel Defoe wrote of Chesterfield: "Here is, however, nothing remarkable in this town but a free school, and a very good market, well stored with provisions, for here there is little or no manufacture..." How the latter change.

By the end of the 19th century Chesterfield had grown to become Derbyshire's second biggest town by which time it possessed three railway stations. To the east and north grew numerous smaller towns and villages, some mere hamlets expanding as a result of new industry, others built from scratch by coal owners and iron masters to house their workers. Great names of industry would dominate - such as The Staveley Coal & Iron Co., The Sheepbridge Iron & Coal Co., Markham & Co., and the Clay Cross Co.

Completion of its canal in 1777 connected Chesterfield to the River Trent and the outside world. Waggonways were laid connecting coal pits and iron mines around Eckington, Renishaw and Staveley with forges and the canal - embryonic railways had arrived.

When the main line railway age dawned, Chesterfield was perfectly situated alongside the path of what one might argue was the HS2 of its day. The North Midland Railway from Leeds to Derby was part of a vision by the so-called Railway King George Hudson for a fast main line from Yorkshire to London Euston Square. Like HS2, it was mired in controversy. The line's engineer, George Stephenson, insisted that in order to maintain a near straight and level route with a maximum gradient of 1 in 330 it must follow the Rother Valley from Masborough (Rotherham) via Eckington to Chesterfield, thus by-passing Sheffield and annoying, to say the least, that town's big wigs. Despite much venom from Sheffield and even attacks on Stephenson's professional credibility, he had his way and the North Midland began running passenger services

Stephenson insisted on the Rother Valley as the route for the North Midland Railway so that gradients could be kept to a maximum of 1 in 330. The aim was not just fast, direct passenger trains but just as importantly, to move the heaviest possible loads of coal. Even so, the route still required some considerable engineering as seen here at 1.50pm on 6th October 1962 when WD 2-8-0 No. 90722 was passing through a deep cutting while approaching Barrow Hill from the north with a mixed consist of loaded and empty coal wagons. *Robert Anderson*

between Masborough, Chesterfield and Derby on 11th May 1840, and throughout from Leeds on 1st July. From those early days Chesterfield was served by a trunk main line with services to Derby and beyond, to Leeds and, via Hudson's connecting York & North Midland Railway, to York. Sheffield was linked in by connections at Masborough with the Sheffield & Rotherham Railway which Sheffield's leaders built themselves. Four years later, the North Midland merged with the Midland Counties and Birmingham & Derby Junction railways to form the mighty and ever expanding Midland Railway.

For the first 22 years of its existence, the North Midland line remained the only railway through the area, but in December 1861 the Midland opened the line south from Clay Cross to the Erewash Valley creating a route to Nottingham and Trent Junction, establishing an important junction at Clay Cross in the process. Passenger services began using this line on 1st May 1862. By this time, it was evident that the route to London would not be to Euston but directly through Leicester to St. Pancras where the great terminus opened for business in 1868.

At the time of the North Midland's opening, numerous shallow coal pits and drifts were being worked around Chesterfield offering relatively low levels of production which was consumed mainly locally. Indeed, coal and iron deposits were discovered during construction of the railway, especially while digging the 1,784-yard Clay Cross Tunnel. One result was the establishment of coal mines and coke works at Clay Cross by George Stephenson and partners with the aim of converting the locally mined coal into coke for the North Midland's locomotives - in the early days of railways steam locomotives burned coke, not coal. In the event, the Midland Railway switched to Durham coke but Clay Cross, with its iron works and, over time, no less than nine collieries, grew into a large complex standing with the growing town, above the tunnel.

By the 1860s, developments in mining techniques saw new deep coal mines being sunk further east which would produce hitherto unheard of amounts of coal that would need moving. Initially, some used their own tramways to connect with the Midland Railway's lines but before long the Midland would provide its own branches by acquiring and upgrading the colliery lines. Among such lines were those to Sheepbridge iron works and collieries; the Brampton branch in Chesterfield; the Springwell Colliery line, going west from Barrow Hill; and the line to Unstone mines, Dronfield.

Meanwhile, an important development took place in 1870 - one which no doubt brought ironic applause from Sheffield. The Midland had finally taken on the challenging topography separating Chesterfield from its Yorkshire neighbour and completed its direct line to Sheffield on 1st February. It branched from the original North Midland route at Tapton Junction, 3/4-mile north of Chesterfield station. The original route would forever be known as the "Old Road." Civil engineering challenges to be overcome included

Clay Cross became an important railway junction upon opening of the line south to the Erewash Valley in 1861. This somewhat dismal scene looking south shows a two-car Derby Works DMU calling there shortly before closure in January 1967. *Railway Station Photographs*

Chesterfield's second station, built by the Midland Railway in 1870 to replace the smaller North Midland original upon completion of the direct line to Sheffield via Dore. Ornate ironwork, bowler hats and milk churns complete the scene in this late Victorian postcard view looking south. *Ray Woodmore collection*

Broomhouse Tunnel, a viaduct over the Drone Valley at Unstone and a five-mile slog at 1 in 100 from Sheepbridge up to Bradway Tunnel, the most formidable works on the line. The navvies digging the 1 mile 267 yard tunnel faced water flooding in at a fearsome rate and millions of gallons had to be pumped out so that work could continue. When the new line opened, it came with a new, larger station for Chesterfield in place of the more modest but attractive Jacobean-style original.

South east of Chesterfield deep coal mines were coming on stream, the large Grassmoor mine having been sunk in 1861. To tap the substantial traffic they would be producing the Midland in 1871 opened a loop line from Avenue Crossing(Hasland) to Pilsley(Morton Sidings) on the Erewash Valley line. It would directly serve Grassmoor, Bond's Main, Lings, Alma, Holmewood, Willamthorpe and Morton collieries. To provide the necessary motive power Hasland engine shed opened four years later. In 1874 the main line between Tapton Junction and the Erewash Valley was quadrupled by the addition of Up and Down goods lines.

By this time a busy rail network had grown up around Chesterfield, but there was more to come - much more. East of Staveley the Midland took over more colliery lines and formed routes from Barrow Hill to Elmton & Creswell via Clowne, and from that line at Seymour Junction to Bolsover, which were opened in 1888. Two years later the Bolsover branch was extended to Pleasley and although these were to be primarily mineral lines the Midland inaugurated Chesterfield-Mansfield passenger services via both routes in September 1890. The Clowne branch would serve Seymour, Oxcroft, and Barlborough(between Oxcroft and Clowne) collieries, while the Doe Lea line to Pleasley would serve Markham, Bolsover and Glapwell Collieries.

For half a century the Midland Railway enjoyed a complete monopoly of the area, but a competitor from the north had been eyeing the riches that the coal and iron industries of the area had to offer. The first incursion by the Manchester, Sheffield & Lincolnshire Railway into what had hitherto been exclusively Midland territory came in December 1891 when it opened a goods branch from Beighton to Staveley iron works. Not too worrying for the Midland perhaps, but by 4th June the following year it had extended the line into Chesterfield, opened a station almost alongside the Midland's - and it was now carrying both goods and passengers. By October it had opened a goods line from Staveley to Annesley Sidings, north of Nottingham, where it linked with the Great Northern Railway, introducing a passenger service to the GN's terminus at Nottingham London Road on 2nd January 1893.

During the course of building these lines, the MS&L laid connections to every colliery along the way. Four left the main line at Staveley where it established sorting sidings, a locomotive depot and houses for its workers. Later in 1893 it extended the Chesterfield branch to the Staveley-Annesley line at Heath, creating the so-called Chesterfield Loop.

All this was happening while the Midland literally looked the other way - towards the west and Manchester in fact when it took direct control of the underfunded Dore & Chinley Railway scheme. The line opened to goods on 6th November 1893 and passenger services on 1st June 1894.

At Chinley, it joined the Midland's existing route from Derby to Manchester and included both north and south facing junctions at Dore. The Hope Valley line, as it would be known to this day, provided the Midland with a Sheffield-Manchester route in direct competition with the MS&L's Woodhead line.

Threading its way between the heights of the Peak District, the Hope Valley line avoided the worst of gradients but some tough stretches were unavoidable including a gruelling five-miles at 1 in 100 from Hope to Edale. It also required two of the longest and deepest tunnels ever built in this country - not counting underground railways and the Channel Tunnel of course - when it came up against hills that it could not circumvent. First, Britain's second longest - the 3-mile 950 yard Totley Tunnel under the 1,227ft Totley Moor, and then the 2 mile 182 yard Cowburn Tunnel - the 9th longest - through hills rising to 1,675ft. between Edale and Chinley and in which is the line summit. Chinley station was re-sited and expanded to deal with its new role as an important cross-country junction.

The MS&L wasn't the only rival muscling in on the scene. A new company had been formed with the intention of building a trans-Pennine route via Chesterfield and Lincoln which would connect Liverpool with a new deep water port on the Lincolnshire coast at Sutton-on-Sea. This was the Lancashire, Derbyshire & East Coast Railway (LD&EC) whose promoters included local coalowner Wiliam Arkwright. It failed to attract backing for the whole route, notably the most difficult part through the Peak District. However, the Great Eastern Railway, looking to cash in on the movement of coal to London, was happy to lend its support. Already as far north as Lincoln by means of its joint line with the Great Northern, the GER, which also had interests in the forthcoming Sheffield District Railway connecting the "Old Road" via Tinsley with the Sheffield-Rotherham line, saw the LD&EC as a means of accessing both Derbyshire coal and the steel riches of Sheffield. Thus, the Chesterfield-Lincoln section duly opened for business in 1897, along with a line from Langwith Junction to Killamarsh giving access to Sheffield which followed in 1898. Its construction required a substantial viaduct over the MS&L and the Midland lines in Chesterfield as well as Duckmanton Tunnel and the 1 mile 864 yard Bolsover Tunnel - Britain's 19th longest. A branch was also laid to Markham and Bolsover collieries.

With all these rivals muscling in, one can imagine the anguish in the Midland's boardroom, but what was about to come must have caused much gnashing of teeth among the Midland directors. This was, of course, the MS&L's London Extension which incorporated the company's existing Beighton-Annesley line besides construction of a

The Midland Railway monopoly of Chesterfield's railways came to an end in 1892 when the Manchester, Sheffield & Lincolnshire Railway entered the scene and rather cheekily opened its own station practically next-door to the Midland's. B1 4-6-0 No. 61313 arrives at the MS&L station - called Chesterfield Central since 1907 - with the 10.5am Sheffield Victoria-Nottingham Victoria at 10.48am on Sunday 3rd November 1957. *David Holmes*

new main line south of Nottingham to London where it would terminate at Marylebone station. With it came the end of the MS&L. It changed its provincial name to the Great Central Railway, reflecting its new national status. The line was completed throughout in March 1899 and from that month, Great Central expresses, coal and goods trains, could run all the way between Manchester, Sheffield, Nottingham, Leicester, Rugby and Marylebone in direct competition with the Midland. Upon completion of a line from Woodford (Buckinghamshire) to Banbury it also had direct access via the Great Western Railway to South Wales and the West Country.

In 1907 the GC absorbed the LD&EC, laid an impressive flying junction at Duckmanton connecting it to the main line, renamed the LD&EC Chesterfield terminus Chesterfield Market Place, its own station Chesterfield Central, and the area's railways were at their zenith.

There was one other to come, however. This was the 71/2-mile 60cm gauge Ashover Light Railway which opened in April 1925 using surplus First World War equipment. Its purpose was to carry limestone from quarries near Ashover directly into the Clay Cross iron works. It also had a passenger service which proved popular with hikers and day trippers in the summer since it passed through the scenic Amber Valley. But the year round service fell victim to bus competition and the remaining summer only service was withdrawn in 1936. The line continued carrying goods and minerals until March 1950 when it closed altogether.

Passenger services

Anyone starting a long-distance train journey from Chesterfield would almost certainly have headed straight for the Midland station where express services ran directly to virtually all parts of Britain. Only to Manchester and the North West were there no direct trains; until modern times that journey usually involved a change at Dore & Totley. Central station, on the other hand, could offer a limited direct service to Manchester over the Great Central lines. By and large, the two main trunk routes through the area mirrored each other's services almost exactly.

The opening of the North Midland may have provided Chesterfield with a convenient route to the south, but reaching near neighbour Sheffield was initially something of an ordeal. At first it involved by-passing Sheffield and then changing trains at Masborough(Rotherham.) When the MS&L opened to Sheffield in 1849 the Midland was able to establish a less indirect route via Beighton. But then 1870 brought a real step change. The new Midland line south from Sheffield and its new station in Sheffield put Chesterfield on a direct express route to West Yorkshire and the North via the steel metropolis. Even then a few prime expresses still took the "Old Road" and missed Sheffield. Opening of the Settle & Carlisle in 1876 added Scotland to the route. Then, in 1879, completion of the Swinton & Knottingley Joint line by the Midland and North Eastern railways gave a more direct route to York and the North

The arrival of the LD&EC in Chesterfield created this stunning three-level railway scene captured by an unknown photographer where its lofty 700ft long viaduct passed over the Midland main line which in turn passed over Mansfield Road. An LD&EC train is departing its Chesterfield terminus and is just crossing a brick arch which advertises the line as "The Dukeries Route." In the foreground the Midland main line passes over the GC Chesterfield Loop. *Stephen Chapman archive*

East. The infrastructure was in place for Chesterfield to enjoy arguably all the services it needed.

Available space precludes a detailed historical analysis of services in the area. In the last year of the Midland Railway's existence, immediately before it became part of the London Midland & Scottish Railway at the 1923 Grouping, the summer 1922 Bradshaw's Railway Guide shows Chesterfield served by just over 70 Midland trains each weekday. Of these 17 were southbound expresses to such places as St. Pancras, Bristol, Bournemouth, Birmingham and Gloucester, 14 ran northbound to Sheffield, Leeds, Bradford, Edinburgh, Glasgow, Newcastle, and Heysham. Many conveyed through carriages to and from places not directly served, including Aberdeen, Halifax, and Harrogate. Another 22 expresses passed through non-stop, some taking the "Old Road" and missing out Sheffield, including three Anglo-Scottish sleeper trains each way.

The Anglo-Scottish trains were branded Scotch Express, the Bradford/Leeds-St.Pancras trains were "Bradford and Leeds Express," and the trains to and from the South West were West Country Express. The St. Pancras-Heysham train (calling Chesterfield at 8.8pm when required to set down) was titled The Belfast Boat Express, the 1.10pm St. Pancras-Leeds(non stop) The Yorkshire Express, and the 11.50pm St. Pancras-Leeds (departing Chesterfield at 3.52am) The North Express. The remaining services were made up of stopping and semi-fast trains between a variety of origins and destinations with Sheffield-Chesterfield-Nottingham/Derby at the core. There were at this time no through trains on the Midland between Chesterfield and Manchester, connections being shown at Dore & Totley.

There were also seven stopping trains from Chesterfield to Sheffield Midland serving intermediate stations along the "Old Road," and six the other way plus an 8.11am from Eckington & Renishaw, while a Saturdays Only 10.48pm from Sheffield provided for those having a night on the town. Some of these trains ran via Treeton and Holmes (Rotherham) and others via the Sheffield District Railway. Two ran each way on Sundays. Chesterfield-Mansfield trains used the "Old Road" as far as Barrow Hill & Staveley Works station. Three ran each way on weekdays via Clowne, one starting at Barrow Hill Monday-Friday, plus two more each way on Saturday evenings. The service on the Bolsover line was very similar. Neither line had a Sunday service.

Although Manchester-Sheffield-Marylebone expresses formed the core of its principal services, the Great Central main line also carried long-distance trains and through carriages between a wide variety of origins and destinations. For instance, from its earliest years, it conveyed through carriages between Manchester and Deal in Kent. Then there was the sleeper between Aberdeen and Penzance, possibly the country's longest run by a single train, and the time-honoured Newcastle/York-Bournemouth

Hasland's 2P 4-4-0 No. 40557 waits with a stopping service in Chesterfield Midland's south end bay on 23rd April 1953 as Bristol Barrow Road Jubilee 4-6-0 No. 45699 *Galatea* turns on the clag while working a South West express. *R.E.Vincent/Transport Treasury*

service. In their day, the GC expresses were notable for speed and comfort, being advertised by such timetable descriptions as Restaurant Corridor Express, or Breakfast Car Express. Alas, this meant little to Chesterfield as most ran non-stop between Sheffield and Nottingham, passing by on the main line directly between Staveley and Heath, although until 1916 Chesterfield was served by a slip coach dropped off the 6.20pm Marylebone-Bradford at Heath. Chesterfield had to make do mostly with Nottingham-Sheffield stopping services, many of them all-stations.

In July 1922 when the GC was still only 23 years old and immediately before the 1923 Grouping when it became part of the London & North Eastern Railway, just five expresses served Chesterfield each day, none from London, and only one to London - the 3.40pm Manchester London Road-Marylebone at 5.21. The only other long distance expresses calling at Chesterfield Central were the 8.55am Sheffield Victoria to Weston-Super-Mare and its return, calling at 9.21am and 3.9pm respectively. These were augmented by Leicester-Manchester Central trains, northbound at 9.9am and southbound at 9.10pm. The backbone of the stopping service was five Nottingham-Sheffield trains each way, plus five from Chesterfield to Sheffield and four from Sheffield, some trains extending to/from Heath on Saturdays when there was also a 10.50pm to Tibshelf Town. Besides these were two all stations trains from Leicester Central and the 5.18pm Leicester-Cleethorpes calling at 6.44. In total there were 17 northbound trains from Chesterfield Central on weekdays(18 on Saturdays) and 14 southbound(17 on Saturdays.)

Those long distance expresses which passed by two miles to the east of Chesterfield along the main line consisted of the 8.20am Manchester-Marylebone and 11.21 Sheffield-Marylebone Luncheon Corridor Expresses, the 10.13am York-Bournemouth Restaurant Corridor Express, the 9.30am Newcastle-Swansea, the 3.26pm Sheffield-Marylebone Restaurant Corridor Express with through carriages from Barnsley, a Glasgow/Edinburgh/Scarborough-Southampton Restaurant Car Express which left Sheffield at 4.17pm and connected with steamers to Le Havre and the Channel Islands, the 4.55pm Bradford Exchange-Marylebone Dining Car Express, the Aberdeen/Glasgow/Edinburgh-Penzance sleeper, the10.3pm York-Bristol and the 9.30pm Liverpool Central-Marylebone mail.

Northbound were the celebrated 2.32am Marylebone-Sheffield newspaper/passenger train, at one time having the second fastest point to point booked time in Britain, the 8.45am Marylebone-Manchester Breakfast and Luncheon Corridor Express, the 10am Marylebone-Bradford Exchange Luncheon Corridor Express, the 10.50am Oxford-York and Scarborough Restaurant Corridor Express with through carriages from Southampton to Scarborough, Edinburgh and Glasgow, the Swansea-Newcastle Restaurant Car Express, the 12.15pm Marylebone-Manchester Luncheon Corridor Express, the 12.3pm Bournemouth to York Restaurant Corridor Express with through carriages to Newcastle, the 3.20pm Marylebone-Halifax Restaurant Corridor Express, the 6.20pm from

A typical Great Central main line express of the late 1950s. Grubby B1 4-6-0 No. 61291 heads an Up train through Renishaw Central on Saturday 12th September 1959. As 61291 is a York engine the train may be a cross-country service. The reporting number 212 is chalked on the smokebox door. The goods yard is on the left while iron ore wagons await transfer to the neighbouring iron works. *Neville Stead collection/Transport Library*

The "Director" class 4-4-0s were prime power for GC line expresses in the 1920s and 30s until Gresley's B17 4-6-0s came along but they were near the end of their days by the time of this picture. A rather workworn D11/1 No. 62663 *Prince Albert* restarts a Sheffield-bound stopping service away from Staveley Central on Easter Monday 30th March 1959. *Neville Stead collection/Transport Library*

Marylebone to Bradford Exchange Corridor Express with through carriages to Barnsley, the Penzance-Glasgow/ Aberdeen sleeper, the Swindon to York due Sheffield at 1.16am, and the 10pm Marylebone to Liverpool Central newspapers/mail destined to become the last train to run throughout from Marylebone to Sheffield.

The fast running of GC line trains, incidentally, was achieved south of Nottingham. North of Nottingham the GC was beset throughout its time by speed restrictions due to mining subsidence. The Midland was similarly afflicted but, passing through the older, more westerly coalfield where mining was ending, settlement was becoming less of a problem.

The Great Central also connected Chesterfield with Mansfield and beyond by means of its LD&EC acquisition from Market Place station. There were six weekday departures from Chesterfield with four extra on Saturdays. The 10.15am and 3.55pm ran the full length to Lincoln. Two others and two of the Saturday extras ran to Mansfield, one plus a Saturday evening extra to Bolsover, one to Warsop(to Mansfield on Saturdays,) and one Saturday evening train to Langwith Junction(renamed Shirebrook North in 1924.) Seven weekday trains came into Chesterfield Market Place, two from Langwith Junction to start the day, three from Lincoln and one from Mansfield. Two Saturday extras ran from Mansfield and one from Bolsover. There was no Sunday service.

With the 1923 Grouping out of the way and the hangover from the First World War receding, the new companies confidently strode forward into what has often been described as the "Golden Age" of rail travel. In 1924, the LNER introduced a King's Cross - Sheffield Pullman which ran via Nottingham and the GC. It was not a commercial success and after rerouting via Retford it was withdrawn the following year.

The 1920s saw the LMS name its principal "Scotch Expresses" The Thames-Clyde Express and The Thames-Forth Express, and the Bradford-Paignton express The Devonian. It also launched The Yorkshireman, the 9.10am Bradford Exchange-St. Pancras and 4.55pm return.

On the GC, Nigel Gresley's handsome B17 4-6-0s began regularly working principal expresses from 1936 in place of the old Great Central engines. Then in 1938 the GC almost achieved motive power parity with the East Coast main line when A1/A3 Pacifics and V2 2-6-2s took over the heaviest and most important London trains. The LMS started replacing the Compound, Class 3 and 2 4-4-0s which had double headed Midland expresses with class 5 and 5XP 4-6-0s.

But dark clouds were gathering. Economic depression and increasing bus competition led to the withdrawal of many local passenger services around the country and among these were the trains between Chesterfield Midland

The ultimate in motive power for any line through the Chesterfield area came from 1938 when Gresley's A1/A3 Pacifics were introduced to the most important expresses on the GC, with *Flying Scotsman* itself among them in the early 1950s. This is A3 No. 60111 *Enterprise* on relatively menial duty leaving Staveley Central with the 7.32am Leicester Central to Manchester London Road via Chesterfield on Friday 6th September 1957. The Pacifics worked on the GC until that month when they were transferred back to the East Coast main line, No. 60111 going to Grantham on 15th September. *Neville Stead Collection/Transport Library*

and Mansfield via Bolsover from 28th July 1930, including closure to passengers of Bolsover, Palterton & Sutton, Glapwell, Rowthorne & Hardwick, and Pleasley stations. And war loomed again. From September 1939 there was no place for glamourous expresses as the movement of troops and supplies took precedence. One prime express to keep running was the Thames-Clyde, but minus such peace-time frivolity as its name.

As we enter the Railway Memories era, we find a railway system battered and worn out by six years of war. It took well over a decade for passenger services to recover to anything even approaching their pre-war standards, a situation perpetuated by ongoing shortages of coal, materials and staff, and a huge maintenance backlog.

The LMS reinstated The Thames-Forth in 1945 but it was much slower than pre-war. On the LNER the popular pre-war 7.30am Breakfast Car Special from Sheffield to Marylebone was revived in 1947 and accelerated to 3 hours 35min. to be the fastest Sheffield-London train by any route (2 hours 50min before the First World War) and named The Master Cutler. Needless to say it did not deviate to Chesterfield Central. Despite its importance, there was often initially nothing better than a B1 4-6-0 to work the 9-coach express and so it had to be decelerated by 12 minutes just to keep time. In the British Railways era especially, the GC main line often suffered inadequate motive power, whether it be under-powered locomotives or locomotives in poor condition. This applied equally to The South Yorkshireman introduced on 31st May 1948 as a revival of the 1930s 10am Bradford-Marylebone express. It was heavily-loaded and although relatively slow it was so popular that a relief was often run. The return of the A3s to the GC - including the celebrated *Flying Scotsman* - improved the motive power situation.

By summer 1946 the LD&EC service from Chesterfield Market Place was little changed from 1922 apart from having fewer Saturday Only trains. The summer service included the Saturday 8.5am Market Place-Skegness and 2.20pm return(arriving Chesterfield at 5.18pm.) Unfortunately, disaster for the LD&EC was not far away, less than seven miles down the line from Chesterfield Market Place in fact. Badly affected by subsidence, Bolsover Tunnel was declared unsafe and had to be closed. Consequently, passenger services were withdrawn from the entire section between Chesterfield and Shirebrook North (excluded) with effect from 3rd December 1951, and the line through the tunnel closed completely along with the stations at Bolsover South and Scarcliffe. Undoubtably, this section of the LD&EC would have lost its passenger service before long anyway.

Since nationalisation in 1948, British Railways had been systematically withdrawing what it deemed to be duplicating services from the company days and a cull of stations in the Chesterfield area and Rother Valley took place between

1951 and 1954 when the remaining "Old Road" local passenger services between Chesterfield Midland and Sheffield Midland, and to Mansfield via Clowne were axed - just one train each way a day on the Clowne branch by 1954. A destination for stopping trains from Chesterfield Midland via Dore was lost in 1952 when Rotherham Westgate closed. By the mid-1950s the only surviving Chesterfield area passenger services were those on the Midland and GC main lines, the Chesterfield loop, and the Hope Valley. Some closed stations were retained for occasional use by excursions or summer Saturday extras.

In 1957, the last year before the GC main line would undergo radical administrative changes that would set it on the road to decline, the summer timetable was much as before, still featuring the line's premier expresses, mainly by-passing Chesterfield as per the norm.

They still included The Master Cutler and The South Yorkshireman as well as the Marylebone-Manchester expresses, the York-Bournemouth, York-Swindon, Friday and Saturday Only Newcastle-Swansea and the overnight Marylebone-Liverpool Central, although the Aberdeen-Penzance sleeper no longer ran. As before, Leicester-Sheffield-Manchester stopping or semi-fast services filled in the gaps, a handful of these trains also avoiding Chesterfield, running direct between Heath and Staveley Central. In fact, one Marylebone-Manchester London Road restaurant car express called at Staveley. Chesterfield continued to be served by mainly stopping services to/from Sheffield and Nottingham or Leicester, plus the one Manchester express.

On the Midland line in summer 1957, The Thames-Clyde Express called at Chesterfield, at 1.7pm northbound but ran non-stop from Sheffield to Trent southbound. The Thames-Clyde, incidentally, became notable for being the only named express on British Railways to carry its name seven days a week. The Devonian called at 11.53 southbound on Mondays to Fridays - on Saturdays it made no advertised stops anywhere between Leeds and Bristol - and 4.39pm northbound. The 9.15am St. Pancras-Edinburgh Waverley called at Chesterfield at 12.11pm(12.20 on Saturdays) and the 10.5am Edinburgh Waverley-St.Pancras at 4.52pm (5.4pm on Saturdays.)

Since nationalisation, operational responsibility for the whole of the GC main line had remained with the LNER's successor, BR's Eastern Region, and that for the Midland main line with the London Midland Region, successor to the LMS. But in 1958 everything south of Pilsley on the GC main line was transferred to the London Midland Region while everything on the Midland line between Horns Bridge, immediately south of Chesterfield, and Skipton went to the Eastern and North Eastern regions. Consequently Chesterfield Midland came to feel rather like a frontier post so far as the railway was concerned.

The LM Region now found itself with two competing and almost identical routes to London. It only needed one and so the eight-year painful rundown of the GC in favour

The Up Thames-Clyde Express, headed by Stanier Class 5 4-6-0 No. 44858, proudly displays its headboard as it coasts through Chesterfield Midland on Thursday 23rd April 1953. *R.E.Vincent/Transport Treasury*

of the Midland began. Having taken away its Pacifics, the Eastern Region switched The Master Cutler to its own King's Cross route via Retford in October 1958, and made it a diesel-hauled Pullman train. The original GC line Master Cutler continued to run, but as the anonymous 7.50am Sheffield-Marylebone restaurant car express and 6.18pm return, as did the other GC line London expresses.

Summer Saturdays were especially hectic in the 1950s and 60s and a look at the summer 1959 timetable illustrates the scale of Saturday traffic at a time when it was virtually at its peak. Universal car ownership and overseas package holidays were yet to make their mark, but the ability to afford two weeks annual holiday at the British seaside during July and August led to a mass movement of humanity every Saturday for just a few weeks as thousands began and ended their holidays on that one day of the week. To cope with this surge in demand, summer Saturdays saw hundreds of extra trains laid on, often formed of elderly carriages unused for the rest of the year. Spare coaching stock retained for peak summer services had to be stored anywhere available, often various wayside locations. The old colliery sidings at Unstone were one such location.

Around 35 extra summer-dated trains were booked to run between Chesterfield Midland and resorts all over Britain on a summer Saturday with another ten passing through non-stop. That's on top of all the regular services, the St Pancras expresses, the Thames-Clyde, The Waverley and The Devonian. What must it have been like for a young spotter on that station on a peak summer Saturday in 1959 with steam-hauled trains one after the other, all day and no desire to be home in time for tea!

They included trains to Scarborough, Morecambe, Blackpool and Filey Holiday Camp from such places as Derby, Leicester, Gloucester, King's Norton(Birmingham,) and Nottingham with corresponding return workings. The 7.30am Sheffield-Skegness via Nottingham called at Chesterfield 8.9-13 then at 8.20 Chesterfield's own seaside special left for Bridlington and Scarborough. The 9.35am Blackpool North-Nottingham, like a number of returning trains, called at Chesterfield to set down only.

Trains to/from what seemed like more exotic resorts many hours away, some overnight, ran between Newcastle and Paignton, Bradford and Bournemouth, Newquay and Newcastle, Weston-Super-Mare and Sheffield, and Teignmouth and Bradford to mention but a few. How the imagination raced with thoughts of the foreign locomotives that would haul these trains later in their journeys - Great Western, Southern, Somerset & Dorset. Besides these were reliefs to the day and night Anglo-Scottish expresses. A few trains missed Sheffield, travelling fast via the "Old Road" while Chesterfield could cock a snook at Sheffield with the southbound Devonian which ran non-stop from Leeds. now arriving Chesterfield at 11.13am. Despite a massive decline in summer Saturday traffic, some of these services would continue in similar form for the next 30 years with Paignton-Newcastle trains being among the country's last loco- hauled summer Saturday extras, running into the early years of the 21st century. A Leicester-Scarborough train still ran in 2018, extended from and to St. Pancras and running to York on Sundays. Summer Saturdays also saw the

The 10.25am Saturdays Only Blackpool-Leicester approaches Chinley at 12.50pm on 25th June 1960 hauled by Royal Scot 4-6-0 No. 46137 *The Prince of Wales's Volunteers(South Lancashire.)*
David Holmes

The last daily passenger trains along the line from Barrow Hill to Elmton & Creswell were withdrawn in 1954 but summer Saturday services continued to use the line. 8F 2-8-0 No. 48127 calls at Clowne & Barlborough, the only intermediate station, with the 10.50am Blackpool-Radford at 3.10pm on 15th August 1959. Goods engines were regularly pressed into passenger service on these manic summer Saturdays.
David Holmes

5.20am unadvertised Leicester-Craigendoran Creative Travel Agents Conference charter and its return working. Summer Saturdays always managed to throw up unusual workings, even in later years, such as 1978 when, for example, the 09.02 Paignton-Newcastle made no advertised stop from Dawlish to Chesterfield.

On the Great Central a summer Saturday was the day when Chesterfield saw far more long-distance trains than at other times with 10 extras calling there. They included the Friday night Sheffield to Hastings and Sheffield to Portsmouth Harbour trains along with daytime trains both ways between Sheffield and Bournemouth and Sheffield and Clacton-on-Sea. Closer to home a Tibshelf Town-Skegness train each way ran via Chesterfield and Worksop. A Central station starter was the 8.14am to Blackpool and 11.20 return which arrived at 3.20pm.

The main line direct between Heath and Staveley saw another 14 additional summer Saturday trains in 1959. They included such long-distance services as the Newcastle-Bournemouth West running non-stop between Rotherham Central and Nottingham, Bradford-Poole extras, and the Hastings and Portsmouth Harbour -Sheffield trains missing out Chesterfield on the northbound journey.

On top of these were the unadvertised cheap fare "Starlight Specials" running on Friday and Saturday nights each way between Marylebone, Edinburgh and Glasgow, the latter originally to/from St. Pancras via the Midland. They were very popular and in the first weekend of the Glasgow Fairs holiday up to a dozen could run from Scotland. Other seasonal overnight trains included the Marylebone-Glasgow and Perth car sleeper services, each running three times a week. Some of these trains were routed via Langwith Junction and the former LD&EC line to Killamarsh. The Midland route also hosted a car sleeper service running between Sutton Coldfield and Stirling. During the 1960s these workings were rebranded Motorail and by 1969 the Midland was carrying overnight Newhaven-Stirling, Newcastle-Newton Abbot and Edinburgh-Newton Abbot Motorail trains.

The 1960s were a time of dramatic change and especially so for Chesterfield's passenger services. As the decline of the GC gathered pace, the LM Region withdrew all through Sheffield-Marylebone daytime trains from 4th January 1960 leaving just the overnight Liverpool mail and news train with its limited passenger accommodation. The South Yorkshireman ceased and was replaced by a Halifax-St. Pancras portion which joined the 8.50am Bradford Forster Square-St Pancras at Sheffield, being conveyed in the return direction by the 5.5pm from St. Pancras.

The Midland line service was little changed by the inter-regional alterations of 1958. In summer 1961, as diesel locomotives were taking over from steam, Chesterfield Midland was served by 19 northbound long-distance expresses in the daytime but just 13 southbound since more of those passed through non-stop. They amounted to four St.Pancras to Bradford trains and three in the other direction along with three Sheffield to St Pancras and two from St. Pancras to Sheffield. The 9.10am St. Pancras to Edinburgh, now named The Waverley, departed Chesterfield at 12.9pm (12.16 on Saturdays)and was followed by the northbound Thames-Clyde at 1.3pm(1.5 on Saturdays.) but in the southbound direction only the Waverley called there, at 5.13pm(5.25 on Saturdays.) The Thames-Clyde called at Chesterfield in both directions on Sundays. The northbound Devonian called there at 4.29pm but southbound it passed through non-stop except on Saturdays when it departed at

The start of the 1960s saw diesels replacing steam on the Midland line expresses. Here, BR/Sulzer "Peak" Type 4 No. D67 eases a Down express past Dronfield Forge where the local pick-up goods had become derailed. *Tom Greaves*

11.18am. At night, the St. Pancras to Glasgow and Leeds sleeper trains both called there while the Edinburgh train passed through without stopping. None of the southbound sleeper services called at Chesterfield.

What we now call Cross-Country, but then known as North East-South West, services had become something of a hotch-potch. Apart from three Bristol-York or Newcastle trains during each weekday, two Newcastle or York-Bristol trains, and two from Bradford to Bristol, each train was unique. A train might run Birmingham-Bradford, Birmingham-Newcastle, Worcester-York, Bristol-Bradford, Cardiff-Newcastle, Paignton-Bradford, Sheffield-Worcester, or Sheffield-Gloucester. The 8.57am Nottingham-Sheffield, departing Chesterfield at 9.38 conveyed through carriages to Hull. Friday nights in the summer saw a succession of overnight trains, six in fact, to Bournemouth, Paignton, Newquay and Penzance.

The Chesterfield Midland local service on Mondays to Fridays in summer 1961 consisted of 20 Up (southbound) trains starting at 6.25am with the 5.50am Sheffield-Nottingham all stations and finishing at 9.58pm with the 6.5pm Bradford-Derby. Most were Sheffield-Nottingham trains but supplemented by Sheffield-Derby trains. Some were semi-fasts calling only at selected stations. The Down service consisted of 16 trains starting at 7am with the all stations Chesterfield-Sheffield and ending the day at 11.9pm with the 10.15pm Derby-Sheffield.

The midweek GC main line local service south of Sheffield stood at 11 Up trains and seven Down, all but one via Chesterfield. They ran variously between Sheffield, Chesterfield, Nottingham and Leicester with two of the Up trains from Manchester and one Down train to Manchester. The one train avoiding Chesterfield, the 6.45am Leicester to Sheffield called instead at Staveley Central at 8.19 having run non-stop from Nottingham. It then called at Renishaw Central and Killamarsh Central. Sundays no longer saw stopping trains on the GC route but some intermediate stations were served by one long-distance express and a limited service of semi-fasts.

By summer 1961, the only mid-week long-distance expresses remaining on the GC line were: northbound the 11.16am Bournemouth-Newcastle, 7.30pm Swansea-Sheffield, 9.40pm Swindon-York, and the 9.55pm Marylebone-Manchester/Liverpool Central. Southbound they were the 8.37am Newcastle-Bournemouth, the 6.40pm York-Swindon(from Scarborough during peak summer,) the 10.22pm York-Swindon and the 9.30pm Liverpool Central-Marylebone. None of these called at Chesterfield. There were a few more cross-country trains on Friday nights including the summer season 9.40pm Newcastle-

Bournemouth complete with restaurant car. Regular overnight trains of note during the early 1960s were the Marylebone-Manchester sleepers, switched from the West Coast main line due to electrification work and Euston station rebuilding. Summer Saturdays remained busy with holiday trains running more or less as outlined previously.

Despite the obvious run-down of GC services, BR stated there was no intention to close the line but that its future lay as a cross-country route via Banbury with freight predominating and not as a London route. Reduction of the Newcastle-Bournemouth restaurant car express to a York-Banbury diesel multiple unit in the winter 1960/61 timetable hardly inspired confidence in this statement. And neither should it have for the run-down continued apace. In 1961 BR proposed withdrawal of all GC line stopping services north of Aylesbury and in 1962 the withdrawal of stopping services north of Nottingham was approved. Thus on 4th March 1963 stopping services between Sheffield and Nottingham were withdrawn and Chesterfield Central closed to passengers along with Staveley Central, Killamarsh Central, Renishaw Central, Heath and Tibshelf Town. The remaining expresses and summer dated passenger trains continued along the main line for a few more years but the GC was finally put out of its misery with effect from 5th September 1966 when they too were withdrawn or, as with the Newcastle-Bournemouth trains, rerouted via the Midland line, which at least meant they now served Chesterfield.

From 18th April that year the Midland main line timetable had been completely re-cast to give hourly regular interval services between Sheffield and St. Pancras, trains alternately running via Derby and Nottingham. Leeds/Bradford trains and the remaining Anglo-Scottish trains were integrated into the Nottingham timetable.

In 2019, the Midland flourishes. With frequent 125mph units on both the St. Pancras and Cross-Country routes and with two Sheffield-Nottingham trains an hour, Chesterfield Midland - just Chesterfield since the closure of Central - is a very busy station. But the Midland didn't reached this happy state of affairs without facing threats of its own.

In 1965, the BR chairman Dr. Beeching, who needs no introduction, unveiled a new plan for pruning the network even further than his notorious 1963 plan. Passenger routes listed for development by 1984 were Sheffield-King's Cross and North East-South West. There would still be a Sheffield-London service via Chesterfield and the Midland of sorts but it would run to Euston via Market Harborough and Rugby or via Nuneaton. The Midland line south of Leicester was not "selected for development" and St. Pancras - unbelievable though it sounds from today's perspective - would close. This "Beeching 2" as it was dubbed, was quietly shelved but not before 1967 when BR revealed that it was considering a Thameslink-style scheme that might have left Chesterfield with no direct London trains. St. Pancras would close and there would be no London trains on the Midland line north of Leicester. Instead a Derby/Nottingham-Euston electrified service would run via Leicester and either Nuneaton or Rugby. Sheffield's London services would be to King's Cross via Retford.

In October 1968 the Midland claimed The Master Cutler when the name was bestowed on the 07.15 Sheffield-St.Pancras and 17.55 return, following withdrawal of the Sheffield-Kings Cross Pullmans which had been losing

The sad scene at Chesterfield Central following closure and removal of the track. The inner relief road was subsequently built on part of the trackbed. *Railway Station Photographs*

Daytime expresses which ran on the GC main line to the very last day were those between York and Bournemouth. The 11.16am from Bournemouth nears Killamarsh at 6.10pm on 26th May 1962 headed by B1 4-6-0 No. 61315. This engine, incidentally, enjoyed an extended life when upon withdrawal from service it became carriage heating departmental loco No. 32 at Nunnery sidings, Sheffield. As such it survived until January 1968 by which time it was the last operating steam loco on BR's Eastern Region. *Robert Anderson*

money just as their 1920s predecessors had. It was not a Pullman but an "Executive" service offering a similar level of service without paying the supplement. By May 1973, it was achieving the fastest time yet between Sheffield and St. Pancras, two and half hours each way, calling only at Chesterfield and Leicester.

The year 1969 saw the Manchester-Harwich boat trains transferred from the Woodhead line to the Hope Valley. That year also saw withdrawal of The Waverley as a general run-down of Midland line London-Scotland services began. The Glasgow sleeper services were rerouted to Euston from May 1969 although they still ran via the Midland. There was another named restaurant car express on the line - the Bradford-Penzance Cornishman but it only called at Chesterfield on summer Saturdays, 09.02 southbound to pick up only and 18.01 northbound in 1973. By 1973 the weekday Leeds-St.Pancras service was just three trains from Leeds and three from St. Pancras, including the Thames-Clyde. Sleeper trains consisted of one St. Pancras-Leeds and a Glasgow-Nottingham; they would soon be withdrawn altogether. By 1978 the Leeds-St. Pancras service was down to just one morning Up train and one from London in the evening. The Thames-Clyde lost its name in 1975 and in 1977 the St. Pancras-Glasgow services were replaced by Nottingham-Glasgow trains. In 1982 these were rerouted via Manchester and the Hope Valley and, to avoid reversal at Sheffield, ran via Beighton and the "Old Road." This left a glaring gap in services between West Yorkshire and the East Midlands so, eventually and after some lobbying, a Nottingham-Leeds service of five trains each way was restored in 1986.

Upon completion of the West Coast main line electrification in 1974, such places as Manchester, Liverpool, Birmingham, Preston and Glasgow were connected to London by what was hailed as the western world's most frequent 100mph service. Two years later, Bristol, Cardiff, Swansea and Bath started to benefit from 125mph InterCity125 services to London. Two years after that the happy citizens of such places as Edinburgh, Newcastle, York, Leeds and Doncaster were being whisked to the English capital at 125mph. Not surprisingly, Sheffield, Chesterfield, Derby, Nottingham and Leicester felt left behind. Their Midland main line trains were still pottering to St. Pancras behind the 90mph "Peak" Type 4 diesels built in 1961 to replace steam and, in some cases, with a time-consuming reversal at Nottingham. Local leaders demanded better. They wanted a share of the InterCity125 revolution.

BR maintained that little speed advantage could be gained with 125s on the Midland line with its curves and speed restrictions and thus, commercially, they were better deployed elsewhere. Better to await electrification and the tilting Advanced Passenger Train, said BR. Electrification north of Bedford, however, wasn't even on the drawing board and we know what became of the APT. Sheffield, Chesterfield and Derby did get InterCity125 services but not where they expected and probably not where they most wanted them. They were introduced on the increasingly important North East-South West route from 5th October 1981 when they replaced loco-haulage on the 07.00 Bristol-Leeds, 08.20 Plymouth-Leeds, 14.37 Leeds-Plymouth and 16.38 Leeds-Bristol. A full HST timetable was implemented in May 1982 with 14 sets making huge cuts in journey times. Ironically, it would take the destructive economic recession of the early 1980s to bring 125s to the Midland main line. BR was forced to review the use of its HST fleet and in October 1982 it transferred six sets to work eight Midland main line services each way, including the Master Cutler - not that they were able to do 125mph over much of it. Among routes to lose some of their HSTs was the North East-South West which consequently retained some Class 47 loco-haulage into the 21st century.

During the 1980s, BR's passenger services came under the control of a new business sector management regime, the London and the North East-South West services came under InterCity, and local services, including those to Chesterfield and the Hope Valley under Provincial Services, later renamed Regional Railways. InterCity immediately undertook a review of the St. Pancras service during which the King's Cross via Retford threat re-emerged. Instead though, it improved standards on the St. Pancras route and from 11th May 1987 the Master Cutler was returned to Pullman status, for marketing purposes at least. North East-South West was rebranded InterCity CrossCountry.

As for local trains, Chesterfield had very few by the late 1960s and it's fair to say that with the remaining small intermediate stations having closed in January 1967, they were hardly necessary. Inter-City and long-distance trains plus the odd Nottingham-Sheffield DMU each way amply provided links with Sheffield, Derby and Nottingham. By 1973 it was served only by the plentiful supply of long-distance trains. In January 1981, however, a revived Sheffield-Chesterfield stopping service of six trains each way was introduced in association with the reopening of Dronfield station under a joint initiative by BR and Derbyshire County Council. Within a few years the dedicated local service was restricted to the morning and evening peaks with Dronfield served the rest of the day by the Leeds-Nottingham trains reinstated in 1986.

For much of its existence, the Hope Valley line was something of a secondary route but until the Second World War and from the resumption of normality in 1946, it enjoyed a reasonable weekday service of stopping trains between Rotherham Westgate, Sheffield, Chinley and Manchester Central or Liverpool Central, interspersed with some fast trains calling only Chinley, Marple, and Stockport Tiviot Dale, and at Dore & Totley to pick up (westbound) and set down(eastbound) connecting Chesterfield passengers.

Looking south from Chesterfield Midland shortly after privatisation towards the former goods station in 1998 with power car No. 43066 on the rear of a St. Pancras-Sheffield HST. The goods warehouses have since been demolished, the train operator Midland Main Line has been superseded by, at the time of writing, East Midlands Trains, while the HSTs themselves are becoming obsolete. *Stephen Chapman*

Until 1914 at least, the 8.30am Manchester-St. Pancras ran via the Hope Valley and the Dore West-South curve while a fast train also ran direct between Sheffield and Buxton via the Chinley East-South curve. A limited service ran on Sundays. But by the mid-1950s, probably as a result of the new Sheffield-Manchester electric service via the Woodhead line, it was reduced to a branch service of Sheffield-Chinley stopping trains with only one remaining fast train westbound. Anyone now wishing to progress to Manchester by this route had to change trains at Chinley, a busy interchange with Manchester/Liverpool-Derby, London and Buxton trains.

All the intermediate stations between Sheffield and Chinley(excluded) were to be closed according to both Beeching's 1963 and 1965 plans and in 1966 the Minister of Transport approved withdrawal of the local service and the station closures. But before the closures could be enacted, things would change. This Hope Valley branch line would buck the 1960s trend - benefiting as it did from both a change of minister and the closure of two hitherto important and, supposedly secure, trunk passenger routes. In 1969 it was awarded a government grant to keep the service running under Section 39 of the Transport Act 1968, as did the remaining Chesterfield-Sheffield local service which was awarded £10,000 for three years.

BR had been questioning the need for five different routes across the central Pennines and so in 1967 it closed the Derby-Manchester line between Matlock and Millers Dale, near Buxton, rerouting its St. Pancras-Manchester expresses via the Hope Valley and the Dore South-West curve. They called at Chesterfield, providing the town with a regular, frequent and direct express service to Manchester. According to the May1969-70 Working Timetable they consisted of five Down loco-hauled trains to Manchester each weekday plus another three DMUs from Nottingham or Derby, the first service of the day starting from Derby and leaving Chesterfield at 08.30. There were four trains to St. Pancras, leaving Chesterfield at 09.19, 13.07, 17.24 and 19.12, plus three Derby/Nottingham DMUs and the 07.00 loco-hauled from Manchester Piccadilly, from Chesterfield at 08.06. A slightly reduced service ran on Sundays. On summer Saturdays at this time the Hope Valley saw Manchester-Yarmouth and Leicester-Blackpool trains.

By 1973, however, the service was down to just two Manchester-St. Pancras trains each way with none on Sundays. And by 1978 they were running only on Sundays when they took up to six hours to complete the London-Manchester journey. It wouldn't be long before anyone wanting to travel between Chesterfield and Manchester would again have to detour via Sheffield.

By the 1980s, the only passenger train booked to use the Dore South-West curve was the 14.25 summer Saturday Blackpool-Leicester DMU. It was withdrawn at the end of the 1981 summer service and the curve became freight only but for the temporary return of Manchester-St. Pancras HSTs in 2003/4 to make up for a reduced Manchester-

The shape of Hope Valley passenger services in the 1950s. Ex-Lancashire & Yorkshire 2-4-2T No. 50646, a resident of Royston shed, calls at Bamford with a stopping service to Sheffield. *R.E. Vincent/Transport Treasury*

Euston service during the West Coast main line upgrading. They swept through Chesterfield, running non-stop between Stockport and Leicester.

Having received the Harwich boats trains in 1969, the next step-up for the Hope Valley came on 5th January 1970 when BR withdrew the Sheffield Victoria-Manchester Piccadilly electric passenger service so that the Woodhead line could be devoted to trunk freight. In its place it introduced an almost like-for-like Sheffield Midland-Manchester class 1 service operated by DMUs running non-stop or stopping only at New Mills; in the 1969/70 timetable the Sheffield service had consisted of just a few stopping trains to Chinley or New Mills. The working timetable from 1st May 1972 shows, in addition to the New Mills all stations service, 14 class 1 DMUs departing Manchester Piccadilly at, as near as possible, xx.45 each hour and Sheffield at basically xx.15 past although the discipline could not be as closely maintained owing to two trains originating from Cleethorpes. The Harwich boat train departure from Manchester was integrated into the regular pattern at 14.40. The last train of the day from Sheffield at 23.25 was loco hauled, as was the 01.50 Manchester Piccadilly-Cleethorpes newspapers.

The summer 1973 timetable shows an increased Sheffield-Manchester service while the Manchester-Harwich boat trains had just been re-routed via Nottingham instead of Lincoln, the train from Harwich now calling at Chesterfield at 11.52; the Harwich-bound train did not stop. Four Hope Valley fast services originated from Hull, one from Scarborough via Hull, and two from Cleethorpes. In the opposite direction three continued to Hull and one to Cleethorpes.

A complete revision of Trans-Pennine services from 14th May 1979 brought further strengthening of the Hope Valley fast service. Class 124 Trans-Pennine units displaced from the Hull-Leeds-Liverpool route were transferred to the Hope Valley along with Class 123 Inter-City sets imported from the Western Region where they were previously in store. The 123s needed extensive restoration at Swindon Works and Lincoln diesel depot to make them fit for public use. The five Hull-Manchester Piccadilly(six on Saturdays) through trains and three the other way were increased to 13 and 10 respectively, while the Cleethorpes service, which had faded to just one train each way, was increased to three from Manchester, remaining at one from Cleethorpes plus one from Doncaster. Before long ordinary DMUs were having to deputise for the worn out Inter-City sets and in May 1984 BR replaced them with loco-hauled trains. Throughout the 1980s the Hope Valley service was in a constant state of flux, being revised year on year. By 1984 the fast service included Nottingham-Glasgow/Edinburgh and Nottingham-Barrow trains each way, plus the Harwich-Glasgow/Edinburgh boat train each way - now a Class 47-hauled InterCity service named The European. In 1986 a Blackpool-Harwich boat train was added.

The following year The European was rerouted via London

The early 1980s era when Inter-City DMUs, redundant elsewhere, were used on Hope Valley fast services. Here, an ex-Western Region Class 123 set heads for Manchester near Hathersage in 1982. Trans-Pennine Class 124 sets were also used on these services, the two types often being combined into hybrid Class 123/124 rakes. *Stephen Chapman*

while the service via Sheffield reverted to a Manchester-Harwich train called The Rhinelander. The Blackpool boat train, meanwhile, had been named The North West Dane. The Manchester-Hull/Cleethorpes trains had largely given way to a Liverpool-Sheffield service. Upon the opening of a new curve at Hazel Grove in 1986 class 1 trains were rerouted via Stockport providing the first direct link with that town for many years.

From May 1988 Class 156 Super Sprinters replaced the loco-hauled trains, the boat trains included, and the North West-East Anglia service pattern of today was born. The stopping service, now operated mostly by the much-troubled Pacer railbuses, was running throughout between Sheffield and Manchester. The new service pattern brought a 40 per cent increase in passengers after only a year and as a result was intensified to hourly Liverpool-East Anglia trains, with two-hourly Blackpool-East Anglia trains while a 450-seat Nottingham- Blackpool loco-hauled train had to be added to cope with demand. The 156s were replaced in the 1990s by the 90mph Class 158s still used in 2019.

In 1994 Regional Railways supported by Derbyshire County Council and the Peak National Park began a more frequent Sunday stopping service in a bid to cut road traffic. It was branded The Hope Valley Explorer and brought back first generation Metro-Cammell DMUs because they could accommodate rucksacks, bikes and push-chairs which the Pacers could not. One set restored to 1960s green livery made frequent appearances. They remained in use on the line into the 21st century when they were among the country's very last first generation DMU workings.

Mention should be made of once major rail traffic which, apart from a handful of overnight mail trains, barely exists nowadays - what were technically referred to as trains formed of non passenger carrying coaching stock, or NPCCS, usually running class C, later class 3 or 4 and consisting mostly of parcels trains. On the Midland, four northbound parcels trains arrived at Chesterfield between 02.52 and 05.28 in summer 1965, remaining there for up to 15 minutes each. Headways could be tight. For instance, no sooner had the 21.45 St. Pancras-Bradford departed at 03.04, than the 20.15 Bristol-Leeds was booked to follow it into the platform at 03.09. Southbound the 00.09 Leeds-Bedford called at Chesterfield from 02.20 to 02.52. Daytime trains were the 10.45 Monument Lane-Sheffield at 13.07-23, and the 03.40 Carlisle-Nottingham, booked to pass through non-stop at 11.27. A few years earlier there had also been the 17.47 Carlisle-Cricklewood milk train. Hope Valley overnight parcels trains in 1969 included Manchester Mayfield-St. Albans, Guide Bridge-Nottingham, and Sheffield-Mayfield trains.

GC parcels trains in the early 1960s included the 8.45pm Marylebone-Liverpool/Manchester Victoria and Preston,

Return of the Manchester-St. Pancras expresses. The 12.47 Manchester-St. Pancras Midland Main Line HST led by an ex-Virgin power car and first coach, is about to pass Earles Sidings, Hope, at 13.27 on Wednesday 25th February 2004. *Stephen Chapman*

and 11.15pm Oldham Clegg Street-Marylebone, diverted from the West Coast main line. Other regulars included the 8.50pm Marylebone-York, and the 5.50am Banbury-York noted in the 1950s for its cargo of rabbit carcasses for northern butchers.

Freight Traffic

From the previous section the impression is rightly gained that there was - and still is - a huge amount of passenger traffic through Chesterfield. But in the past, when this was an area of intense industrial activity - mining, coking, steel making and heavy engineering - freight was dominant. Unglamorous, workaday with grimy uncoloured engines and no fancy names but nonetheless a permanent, or so it seemed then, constantly moving backdrop to not just the railway scene, but to everyday life.

Until the collapse of industry and greater reliance on imports which has plagued Britain over the last half century, the main flow of freight had been a steady procession of Yorkshire, Derbyshire and Nottinghamshire-produced coal and coke southbound to meet the voracious demands of homes and industry in London and the South. Northbound, was a steady flow of iron ore to the furnaces of the North East, North Lincolnshire and South Yorkshire from quarries in the south Midlands, especially from the second world war when home production was stepped up. Likewise were incoming iron ore, limestone, coal and coke for the furnaces at Clay Cross, Staveley, Sheepbridge and Renishaw.

The products of all that effort were the third main source of traffic, iron, steel and steel products such as tubes, manufactured goods of every kind, by-products and chemicals, not least those produced in the immediate area. Of course, there were also all the general, everyday goods and supplies to be delivered, everything from pit props and scrap metal to perishables and cattle, and often over very long distances passing through by strictly timed overnight express freights.

On the Midland lines, endless loads of coal were conveyed to Toton marshalling yard, situated in the Erewash Valley. There they were formed into block trains for London hauled from the late 1920s by the monster LMS Garratts, ably supported by Stanier's 8F 2-8-0s from 1935 and then replaced in the 1950s by BR's powerful 9F 2-10-0s. On the Great Central lines coal for the south was similarly worked to Annesley yard where it was gathered into block loose-coupled trains given leave to travel at up to 50mph over the GC main line to Woodford yards, situated in the Buckinghamshire countryside. These celebrated "Windcutters" or "Runners" as they became known, were worked by class 01 and 04 ex-GC 2-8-0s when first introduced in 1947 but from the 1950s they too became the preserve of the 9Fs.

The Hope Valley line also had its share of heavy mineral traffic with coal and coke going through the Peak District

The LMS Garratts which plied the Midland line from the 1920s to the 1950s must have been quite a sight to behold. No. 47986 heads a heavy mineral train southwards through Chesterfield Midland in the early 1950s. Evidently the protruding elbow from a neighbouring photographer was as much a problem then as it is today. *Tom Greaves*

to Gowhole yards, just east of New Mills, for onward movement to Manchester and other North West industrial centres. Stone and cement traffic from the Peak District came the other way but back in steam days it had yet to reach today's colossal proportions.

Using the summer 1963 working timetable for this survey, there was something like 400 freight train movements in or through this area on the Midland and Great Central systems combined every 24 hours during the week.

Both systems saw long-distance freights - many fully braked express services running mainly during the night - and middle distance trains. A plethora of local trip workings plied between local yards, the various collieries and industrial plants almost entirely during the day, bearing in mind that the day often began at 5am. Focal points for the bulk of this traffic were Barrow Hill, Seymour Junction, a small yard at Hollis Lane, next to Chesterfield station, and Avenue Sidings on the Midland, and Staveley Central on the GC. On the Midland, most freight travelled via the "Old Road" but there was a steady flow over the Hope Valley. Only a handful of trains ran to and from Sheffield via Dore. It should be noted that freight operations were very different on Mondays and Saturdays to those about to be mentioned. Many trains did not run on Monday mornings or were retimed to run later. On summer Saturdays and Friday evenings some trains were suspended to leave capacity and resources for the heavy holiday traffic of that era. This applies to the Midland and GC systems alike.

The GC lines saw in the region of 120 freight workings per 24 hours, including some 30 local trips. Almost a hundred were the hard working, unglamorous unbraked, loose-coupled class 8s, more often than not in the hands of the robust and functional O4 and O1 2-8-0s. The long and middle distance trains came from a wide variety of origins and went to a wide variety of destinations. From Staveley they ran to Mottram, Wath, Worksop, Frodingham, Immingham, York, Grimsby, Hull, Ickles, (Rotherham) and Broughton Lane(Sheffield.) Mostly these were the odd train to and from one place or the other but eleven ran to Annesley each 24 hours conveying coal rounded up at Staveley from local pits.

Apart from the odd train from Annesley and New Hucknall, almost all incoming class 8s terminating at Staveley came from the north: Wath, Dewsnap, Sheffield Bernard Road,Worksop, Stockton, Kiveton Park, York, Moor Road, Ickles, and Mansfield via a reversal at killamarsh. Besides these were longer distance class 8s passing through, detaching and attaching wagons at Staveley while others stopped only for water, or engine and crew changes. They included trains from Woodford to Tees, Frodingham and Renishaw, from Annesley to Mottram which would change from steam to electric haulage at Rotherwood for their journey over the Pennines, and Annesley to Immingham, and from Worksop, Sheffield Bernard Road, Stockton, Frodingham, Ickles and Normanby Park(Scunthorpe) to Annesley. Among them were block steel loads from Consett and Scunthorpe to South Wales. A coke train ran from Smithywood coking plant to Renishaw for the iron works; there was a train from Cudworth to Stanton Works, and oil tanks from Stanlow refinery, Cheshire, to Colwick.

Six class 4 fully braked express freights with vacuum

WD 2-8-0 No. 90318 passes Barrow Hill Junction signal box while heading a Down class 8 goods along the "Old Road" on Tuesday 16th October 1962. *Robert Anderson*

Everyday freight on the GC lines. Class O4/3 2-8-0 No. 63656 skirts the Chesterfield Canal near Staveley Works on the Chesterfield Loop with a Down coal train at 12.45pm on Saturday 28th April 1962. No. 63656 was one of those members of the class supplied to the army's Railway Operating Division for First World War service and taken into railway stock after the war. The Chesterfield Canal, like most others, came to be owned by the railway, in this case the Manchester, Sheffield & Lincolnshire(subsequently the Great Central) which was then able to divert it between Killamarsh and Eckington to enable construction of a straighter railway. *Robert Anderson*

brake operating throughout the train passed through Staveley, mostly at night: 4N26 3.32am Woodford-Hull; 4N22 4.40pm(5.30 on Saturdays) Woodford-York; 4M26 1.30am Hull-Annesley; 4M21 3.10am Dringhouses-Woodford; 4V21 12.55am Tees-Cardiff "The Welshman;" and 4V23 2.25am Tees-Bristol "The Bristol." This does not seem many for the GC main line and that is because quite a number of overnight express freights were routed via Langwith Junction and Killamarsh. There were also six class 5 express freights(operating vacuum brake fitted on at least half the vehicles): 5E32 9.15pm Leicester Goods-Sheffield Bernard Road; 5E76 1.30am Woodford-Sheffield Bridgehouses; 5E77 8.20pm Annesley-Wadsley Bridge; 5N38 5.53pm Woodford-Ardsley; and 5M25 8.5pm Manchester Ardwick-Woodford. Just two partly fitted class 6 trains were booked via Staveley: 6M48 9.35pm Dewsnap-Annesley and 6M26 Mexborough Top Yard-Annesley. There were also four unfitted class 7 trains: 7N58 3am Staveley-York; 7E13 1.55am Annesley-Kiveton Park Colliery; 7M77 10.55pm Ardsley-Annesley and 7E95 11.25pm Staveley-Colwick. Seven local trip diagrams were booked from Staveley serving the various collieries, foundries and depots(see page 99.)

During a normal mid-week 24 hours, freight trains over the Hope Valley averaged one each way every hour, with 23 Down trains and 24 Up trains. At the eastern end most trains originated from Avenue Sidings, between Hasland and Clay Cross which were the exchange sidings for colliery traffic from the Pilsley loop as well as the enormous Wingerworth coking plant. Most Down trains were class 8 from Avenue with a couple from Tibshelf or Toton and a few from Barrow Hill, the latter reversing at Tapton Junction. Most went to Gowhole Yard where they were remarshalled for onward delivery to their final destination though some extended through to such places as Trafford Park or Cheadle Junction. The 10.38 and 11.5am class 8s from Avenue went to Earles Sidings at Hope, the exchange sidings for the private branch line to Earles' cement works, the return empties booked to leave for Avenue at 6.48am. In the Up direction, many trains were class 7 empties. At the east end the odd class 7 or 8 train went on to Blackwell, Westhouses or Toton, some originating from Heaton Mersey or Cheadle Junction. Class 6 partly fitted freights in the Down direction included two trains of empties from Tibshelf to Trafford Park. Worth a mention are 6M20, the 11.22pm Chesterfield-Gowhole and 8E35, the 3.33am Gowhole-Chesterfield.

Hope Valley freights to and from the Sheffield direction included the line's only class 4 fully fitted, 4E15, the 6.15pm Gowhole-Masborough. Class 6 trains were 6N01 the 12.25am Heaton Mersey-Hunslet; 6E86 the 10.5pm Walton Sidings-Sheffield Engine Shed Sidings; and 6M19, the 9.10pm Masborough Sorting Sidings-Walton. There

Gowhole Yard, between Chinley and New Mills, was the western start and finish point for many Hope Valley freights. A Manchester Centrall-Sheffield service headed by B1 4-6-0 No. 61152 is seen passing between the groups of sidings in 1961. A train of empties on the right is headed by a pair of Eastern Region engines but one wonders what the occasion was on this particular day as there are three trains of empty passenger stock with engines on at the far end in the sidings on the left. Could they be Belle Vue excursions stabling while their happy trippers visit the zoo? *Neville Stead collection/Transport Library*

were also a few class 7 and 8 trains, some with limestone from Buxton area quarries.

This all sounds very hectic but now we come to the busy part. The amount of freight on the Midland main line back in summer 1963 was just mind-boggling. So much so that it is difficult to know where to start or whether it is even wise to attempt to describe it in any detail. But here goes. Each 24 hours mid-week there were just short of 200 booked freights ranging from class 4 right down to the humble class 9 - a freight train on average every seven minutes, though not all actually ran through Chesterfield. Forty four were class 4 fully fitted expresses, a few of which ran via Sheffield, mainly during the night. There were half a dozen class 5 partly fitted trains, a similar number of class 6, 26 class 7 and no less than 108 unfitted class 8 goods and mineral trains. Five ran class 9 - booked to shunt mid-section at wayside sidings as they ambled along their way.

The premier freights on the Midland line at this time were the 7.23pm Hendon to Gushetfaulds(Glasgow,) and the 7.50pm, Gushetfaulds Hendon block container trains - "The Condor." So prestigious were they that they were class 3, 3S60 northbound and 3M29 southbound. They represented the future for general freight and were the fore-runners of today's Freightliner services, and as such diesel-haulage was compulsory. Therefore, they were entrusted to pairs of troublesome MetroVick Co-Bos which sometimes had to be replaced by something more reliable, such as a steam engine. The northbound train was timed to pass Chesterfield at 10.37pm and ran via Sheffield while the southbound train, due at 2.27am, ran via the "Old Road." There was one other class 3, the 9.15pm York-Birmingham fish(3M15,) via Sheffield and passing Chesterfield at 12.28am(12.48am on Sunday mornings and 11.56pm on Sunday evenings.

Notable among the class 4 express freights were those that ran between Water Orton and Carlisle, worked throughout by 9Fs and men from Birmingham's Saltley depot. Fully fitted heavy iron ore trains from Wellingborough to Teesside, also 9F-hauled as far as York, were class 4. Of the others there were almost as many origins and destinations as there were trains. But as examples, they ran from Lawley Street (Birmingham) to Hunslet and York; from Somers Town(London) to Hunslet and Hull; St. Pancras to Bridgehouses; Willesden and Leicester to Carlisle; Bristol to Dringhouses; Tyne Yard to Lawley Street; Glasgow, Carlisle, Bradford and Sheffield Wicker to St Pancras and Washwood Heath (Birmingham;) Hurlford(Kilmarnock) to Brent - a train conveying everything from carpets and woollen goods from the mills of Catrine to explosives from the ICI works at Ardeer; York Dringhouses and Stourton to Washwood Heath; Carlisle to Stoke Gifford; Bradford and Stourton to Westerleigh Junction, plus another fish train, 4M78 the 1.28am

A fully fitted class 4 express freight, possibly 4M51 the Friday Only 5.45pm Glasgow-St. Pancras running 37 minutes ahead of time, rolls southbound through Barrow Hill behind Derby-allocated "Black Five" 4-6-0 No. 45285 at 1.5pm on Saturday 6th October 1962.
Robert Anderson

Sheffield-Birmingham. Since the rivers Ouse and Don were unlikely to yield much in the way of palatable fish, it seems likely that York and Sheffield were marshalling points for loads from such places as Whitby, Scarborough and Hull. Then there were 4S09 and 4M01, possibly the most important trains on the line - the 9.10pm Burton Wetmore-Millerhill and 8.2pm Burton Wetmore-Carlisle beer trains, the latter calling at Chesterfield on Fridays when it ran only to Hunslet. And so the list goes on. A number of class 4 trains were, by this time, being hauled by express passenger locomotives in the form of Jubilee 4-6-0s displaced from the St. Pancras expresses by diesels and concentrated at Burton shed. Not surprisingly they included the Burton-Carlisle/Hunslet beer train as well as 4N33 the Somers Town-Hunslet and 4M87 the 5.12pm Sheffield Engine Shed Sidings-Washwood Heath.

The few class 5 trains followed roughly the same routes, such as St. Pancras and Water Orton-Hunslet and Humberstone Road(Leicester)-Masborough, Stourton-Chaddesden(Derby) and Nottingham. Likewise the class 6 trains, making such journeys as Lawley Street-Normanton and Sheffield Engine Shed Sidings; and Stourton, Normanton and Masborough-Leicester. The 5.25pm trip from Sheffield Nunnery to Chesterfield Hollis Lane, via Dronfield, also ran class 6, due Hollis Lane 6.10pm.

A significant proportion of the class 7 trains were the afore-mentioned empties returning from Gowhole but there was also a Stanford-le-Hope to Heysham oil train which ran as required, due past Chesterfield at 5.27am on Wednesdays and Fridays and 7.11 am on Tuesdays and Saturdays. There were also Toton, Washwood Heath and Rowsley-Barrow Hill workings, Lloyds Sidings(Corby) to Cadeby Colliery and Wath Yard empties, and empties to Seymour Junction from Partington, Rotherham Main coking plant, Northwich, and Sheffield E.S. Sidings. An overnight class 7 from the Scunthorpe area went to Water Orton or Avenue Sidings depending on which day of the week it was. Class 7s arrived at Hollis Lane at 3.15pm(from Eckington & Renishaw,) and 8.59pm(Sheffield Bernard Road, 5.17pm on Saturdays.) Another class 7 was the 5.15am Wincobank Sidings-Renishaw Park Goods.

The class 8 trains, of which there were well over a hundred per 24 hours and which ran mostly during the day, covered very similar routes to those already mentioned as well as working locally. They included those which ran across the Pennines to Gowhole, those which took coal from Barrow Hill and Wath to Toton for forwarding to the south, several Normanton-Chaddesden workings, and those conveying iron ore from Appleby Frodingham company's Ashwell Sidings in Rutland, and Richard Thomas & Baldwins at Blisworth, Northamptonshire, to Frodingham.

The branches going out east towards Mansfield via Elmton & Creswell and Bolsover were served mainly by eleven daytime class 8 trip diagrams with Barrow Hill engines and men, and which had the yards at Barrow Hill or Seymour Junction as their operating hubs. Beyond Oxcoft Colliery traffic on the Clowne branch was light. Other trips worked in from outside the area or from Hasland depot.

In 1956 when Hasland shed came under the Rotherham District Operating Superintendent, it provided power for six trip diagrams. Among other places these worked Avenue Sidings-Dunston & Barlow, Hollis Lane, Clay Cross and along the Pilsley Loop to Grassmoor and Holmewood collieries and Alma Junction. Trip 149 worked the Brampton

With Barrow Hill station in the right background, 4F 0-6-0 No. 44071 is on Target 69 duty at 1.25pm on Saturday 6th October 1962. Barrow Hill goods loading and vehicle dock is in the left background, but the main goods depot, including the goods shed and 10-ton crane, were situated alongside the engine shed. The goods facilities were closed in July 1965. *Robert Anderson*

branch and was specified "Class 3 Tank Engine." As late as 1963 it was still specified "Steam Engine."

It was not long after 1963 that times began to change. The Beeching closures, government legislation enabling BR to opt out of unprofitable traffic, increased concentration on block trainloads, industrial decline, motorways and bigger lorries, declining use of coal, and the progressive closure of local collieries and iron works brought about a reduction in traditional railway freight and the number of freight trains running across the rail network.

The opening of Tinsley marshalling yard in October 1965 brought a significant change in operations locally, being a new origin and destination for many of the through freights and local trips alike. It replaced many of the older small yards dotted around BR's Sheffield Division. The former Midland yards in the Chesterfield area, such as Barrow Hill and Seymour Junction, were retained for dealing with local traffic and were kept busy for as long as there was enough traffic to keep them busy. Through freight traffic on the GC main line was unaffected as it was withdrawn and switched to Midland routes a few months before Tinsley opened. Staveley Central yard and engine shed had closed and collieries along what would soon become the surviving rump of the GC main line to Duckmanton were served by trips from Barrow Hill or Tinsley.

A grim traffic flow in the 1960s by both Midland and GC routes was the sad procession of withdrawn steam engines being towed to Sheffield, Rotherham, and local scrap dealers for cutting up.

By summer 1970 the changes wrought in the 1960s were starting to show. Many local yards had closed while the age of the air-braked block trainload was making itself known. There were still around 200 booked mid-week freights per 24 hours on the Midland lines, all but ten overnight trains running via the "Old Road." But with the GC traffic gone, that's only half the total for the whole area in 1963. The class 8s still predominated and many ran between the same origins and destinations, including Barrow Hill-Toton but also Barrow Hill-Tinsley.

Under a new train classification system based on the train's permitted speed class 8s were restricted to 35mph and included new flows such as Scunthorpe-West Midlands steel terminals. Class 6 trains, of which there were now around two dozen, were timed for a 45mph maximum but included new fully fitted block company trains, such as oil trains and a number carrying limestone from the Peak District which were permitted to run at 60mph. There were just over a dozen class 7 trains, also permitted to run at 45mph, but the number of class 9 trains had grown to almost 50 in total. Restricted to no more than 25mph, the bulk of these were mainly loose-coupled local workings and trips. They included several trips between Markham Colliery and Avenue Sidings.

Booked class 4 trains, now described as "Freightliner, COY and Express Freight Trains timed to a maximum speed of 75mph," amounted to just 4E65, the 01.45 Dudley-Follingsby air braked freight; 4E32, the Tuesdays and Thursdays Only King's Norton-Wakefield company train (cars;) or Wednesdays and Fridays Only King's Norton-Tyne Central Freight Depot company train; 4E66 16.20 Swansea-Sheffield Freightliner (via Dronfield,) 4V60 01.35 Sheffield-Swansea Freightliner (via Dronfield;) 4M47

The grim procession of withdrawn engines destined for scrapyards in the surrounding area was very much part of the 1960s freight scene. These three 4F 0-6-0s - 44265 the nearest - and two 8F 2-8-0s in the closed goods yard at Killamarsh on the "Old Road" were photographed from the cab of a southbound loco by fireman Roy Wood on Sunday 10th May 1964. *Peter Rose collection*

Tuesdays and Thursdays Only 11.54 Wakefield-Longbridge company train; 4M38 Wednesdays Fridays Only Gateshead-Longbridge company train; and 4M61, the 21.04 Follingsby-Dudley. At that time, the notion of a freight train running at 75mph seemed fanciful but they would eventually become the norm. Most of the class 4 trains of old were still running but had become class 6 while the great class 4 iron ore trains to the north were no more since the switch to imported ore. A regular coal flow in the late 1970s/early 1980s was from Bolsover to Chinnor cement works in Oxfordshire. On what remained of the GC lines, coal from Arkwright Colliery was tripped to Barrow Hill.

Freight on the Hope Valley had fallen to about half what it was in 1963. The yards at Gowhole had closed and the traffic they handled dissipated. But the 20-plus freights on the route, almost all at night, represented the start of a new era as most were now to or from Hope Cement works or Buxton area quarries. As with passenger trains, Hope Valley usage benefited when through freight trains were rerouted from the Matlock route in October 1966. From this low, freight would steadily grow.

By summer 1989 the volume of freight traffic in the area had reached a low ebb with just over 80 booked trains through Chesterfield on average per mid-week 24-hours and, as per usual, many ran on some days and not on others. There were only three collieries left that were despatching coal by rail: Markham, Bolsover, and the Oxcroft opencast, plus the Bolsover Coalite works. What coal traffic remained was now in 1,100-tonne Merry-Go-Round trains running direct between the pits and their destinations, usually power stations or steel works relatively far away, or by means of the Speedlink Coal Network using air-braked hopper wagons. The great Avenue coking plant had gone over to "Merry-Go-Round" operation in 1983 reducing the role of Avenue Sidings, and would soon close. There was little use now for the sidings at Seymour Junction or for sorting at Barrow Hill where some sidings have remained purely for stabling purposes. The once ubiquitous class 8 trains, along with the class 9s and the remaining old 16-ton mineral wagons with their loose couplings and clanging buffers were now almost extinct, confined to engineers' trains. Only eight of these were booked in the working timetable.

Class 6 trains now predominated with just over 50 per 24 hours plus just short of 20 class 7s. As well as MGR and SCN coal trains, these included long-distance Speedlink wagonload freights, block steel trains, oil trains, stone trains and various other company trains. There were just five booked class 4 trains which were either Freightliners or automotive services.Trip workings were now few and far between but traffic for the surviving stump of Chesterfield's Brampton branch to the works of Chesterfield Cylinders still required moving and the resident class 08 shunter pushing a rake of bogie bolster wagons over the bridge crossing the Chesterfield relief road which had previously been the GC line remained a familiar sight.

By the year 2000, the surface mine at Oxcroft was the only remaining colliery connected by rail in the Chesterfield area while the coke and by-products plant at Bolsover would soon close. In spite of this there were around a hundred booked freights per 24 hours through

Chesterfield area freight in the 1970s. English Electric Type 3 No. 37295 heads north along the Down Goods line between Chesterfield station and Tapton Junction on Monday 9th July 1979 with a military load consisting of field guns and various vehicles. *Adrian Booth*

Chesterfield in 2019 following a revival driven largely by the growth in container trains carrying all kinds of goods and, most of all, aggregate and cement traffic emanating from the Hope Valley which can see more than 80 freights per 24 hours - twice as many as in 1963. It should be born in mind, however, that according to the system operated nowadays, freights shown in working timetables are actually paths which may not always be used by the operator concerned.

All Change

From their very beginning the railways were built for one purpose above all others - to carry coal and while other factors also drove construction of the principal main lines through the Chesterfield area, the branches from them were built for coal. Consequently they lived and died with the pits they served..

It has been estimated that over time there has been something like 900 coal mines around Chesterfield, ranging from shallow small pits with no railway connection to big, deep shaft collieries and associated coke ovens, brick works, railway installations and, in some cases, ironstone mines. Following nationalisation in 1947 the National Coal Board's East Midlands No.1 Area was the Chesterfield Area which in 1956 still embraced 23 sites including collieries, coke ovens, washeries and by-products plants.

Many older and smaller mines came and went in the 19th century, closing during the 1880s and 1890s due to a slump in the price of coal caused by over-supply. The same scenario would play out a hundred years later during the "Coal Crisis" when prices were forced down by imports and the outcome, enabled by government policy, would be fatal to the industry. As time went on, the north Derbyshire coalfield naturally receded from the west as production became concentrated on the big, modern and profitable pits mining deeper, more productive seams further east.

Coal production in Britain peaked in 1913. The First World War and subsequent international politics resulted in a big drop in coal exports which never recovered, although prices later recovered enough to encourage the reopening of some of the previously closed pits.

Then the internal combustion engine and increasing use of oil contributed to an ongoing decline in demand. Later, such factors as the switch from steam to diesel and electric on the railways, natural gas and other alternatives accelerated the decline. Pit closures and the loss of heavy industry would gain momentum throughout Britain from the 1960s onwards - most especially in the 1980s. The decline was partially offset by increasing demand for electricity which at the time was produced mostly by coal-fired power stations. With the rise of the giant power stations from the late 1960s the coal would have to come from the biggest pits geared up to meet the demand for continuous bulk supplies delivered by the "Merry-Go-Round" method of train operation.

Precise closure dates for many of the freight only lines and mineral branches are difficult to pin down, so the best way to chart the contraction of the North Derbyshire rail network is to chart the reshaping and ultimate decline of coal mining in the region. Rail traffic sometimes continued after a pit had closed because stocks of coal had to be cleared, and also it was not unusual for rail traffic to cease in advance of a colliery closing. Some dates are doubtless open to contradiction as sources often conflict but what is indisputable is the rapid and inexorable extinction of a great industry over the final quarter of the 20th century.

Branches affected by colliery closures in the late 19th century included the Monkwood and Nesfield extensions of the Sheepbridge iron works branch, and the Unstone and Springwell branches. Also closed was Broomhouse Colliery and brickworks, connected to the Dore line by a short branch. Contempory Ordnance Survey maps denote the Nesfield, Monkwood, Unstone and Springwell branches as belonging to the Midland Railway and all were shown in situ for several decades after the colliery closures. Part of the Springwell branch remains to this day as a long siding. Short sections of the Nesfield and Monkwood branches still served slag tips and opencast coal workings in the 1960s. By 1898, however, Ireland, Markham, Bolsover and Glapwell collieries had opened along the Barrow Hill-Pleasley line and Southgate Colliery at Clowne on the Seymour Jn.-Creswell branch. A connection from the GC Chesterfield Loop into Calew and Bond's Main collieries had also opened.

Some restructuring of the network occurred as a result of the Great Central absorbing the LD&EC. An LD&EC branch from its main line east of Chesterfield to Bond's Main Colliery had been completely lifted by 1918 and maybe not even completed before the takeover. It served Hazel Well Colliery and brickworks en-route which had closed in 1914 and 1917 respectively.

Further pit closures affecting the railways had come by the end of the First World War. These included Boythorpe, New Brampton and Riber pits - connected to the Brampton branch, and Lings Colliery at the end of a branch from the Midland's Avenue-Pilsley line. But around the same time, Oxcroft Colliery with a Midland Railway branch from the Seymour Jn.- Clowne line had opened, while a new Unstone Colliery had opened - listed in 1923 as producing coal for "gas and manufacturing." Plumbley Colliery, connected to the "Old Road" at Eckington closed around

The Merry-Go-Round method developed in the mid-1960s became the standard means of moving large loads of coal. On Wednesday 9th April 1980 pioneer Class 56 No. 56001 heads a loaded southbound MGR train past Avenue Sidings where traditional 16 ton mineral wagons are still well in evidence. A pair of Class 20s hide among the wagons while in the left distance can be seen the bridge carrying the branch into Avenue coking plant over the main lines. *Adrian Booth*

1920, Alma Colliery, situated on an incomplete branch from Alma Junction towards Clay Cross, followed in 1922, and Southgate Colliery, Clowne, in 1929. But also in 1929 production began at Hope cement works which would be crucial many years hence in compensating for the loss of coal traffic.

The 1930s saw the opening of Arkwright Colliery which would ensure survival of a small part of the LD&EC main line's Chesterfield end into modern times. New coke ovens were established at Grassmoor Colliery in 1935 and the Derbyshire Coalite plant at Bolsover in 1936. Clay Cross collieries Nos. 2, 3 and 4 were closed by 1939. The 1930s saw the final closure of Unstone Colliery and of the Unstone loop which was absent from the LMS 1935 Sectional Appendix, and of Brampton Colliery, the last on the Brampton branch. Hartington, Seymour and Barlborough collieries all closed during the same period.

The first significant main line closure came in December 1951 when serious geological instability forced the closure of Bolsover Tunnel causing the LD&EC line between Shirebrook North and Markham Junction to close that December. It also brought withdrawal of all passenger services from Chesterfield Market Place as well as cutting off access from the GC main line to Lincolnshire via Langwith Junction. Lincolnshire trains would now have to travel via Killamarsh, the Waleswood curve and Worksop. A similar event affecting Rawthorn Tunnel had resulted in closure of the Barrow Hill-Mansfield Woodhouse line between Glapwell and Pleasley during the 1930s.

Bond's Main Colliery, which had connections to the Avenue-Pilsley branch, the GC main line and the GC Chesterfield loop, had closed by 1953. Avenue Colliery (Clay Cross No.9) and coke ovens, situated on the Down side of the North Midland main line at Wingerworth, just south of Chesterfield, had also closed by 1953 but on the site was built the massive 3/4-mile long Avenue Carbonisation and Chemical Plant which began production in 1956, replacing Grassmoor coke ovens where the colliery had been combined with Williamthorpe in 1950. As well as connections from the Down side, it was linked to Avenue Sidings on the Up side by a branch which bridged the four main running lines. Until 1983 this branch was worked by NCB Coal Products Division's own engines.

Chesterfield Market Place gave up the ghost and closed to goods in March 1957 and the LD&EC line from there to Arkwright Colliery was abandoned completely. Another loss in 1957 was Pilsley Colliery followed by the last of the Clay Cross Pits in 1962.

Before nationalisation of the railways in 1948 each of the private companies had their own connections to many of the collieries as they competed for business. But when they were all brought under British Railways this was no longer

Following the enforced closure of Bolsover Tunnel and withdrawal of LD&EC passenger services between Chesterfield Market Place and Shirebrook North in 1951, Market Place goods yard soldiered on for another six years. This 1950s view shows the abandoned passenger terminus and, on the left. the lingering goods yard. In the left distance is the goods warehouse, on a site which would later be occupied by offices for the Accountant General's Department of the General Post Office. The magnificent neo-classical town hall overlooks the scene. *Railway Station Photographs*

always necessary and so BR began a money-saving programme of single sourcing, cutting out duplication of colliery connections. Local examples of this were the abandonment of the LD&EC branch to Markham and Bolsover collieries and the further cutting back of the LD&EC main line from Markham Junction to Duckmanton. The former Great Central branch to Renishaw Park Colliery which passed over the "Old Road" was also deemed superfluous.

The closures mentioned so far were relatively minor but cataclysmic events were about to remove around half of the local rail network in the space of a few years. On 4th March 1963, local passenger services were withdrawn from the GC main line and, as a result, Chesterfield Central, Staveley Central, and all other surviving intermediate stations between Sheffield and Nottingham, were closed to passengers, and the line from Chesterfield to Heath Junction closed completely. Grassmoor station had closed completely in 1940. Chesterfield suffered another retrenchment in June 1964 when Boythorpe Wharf goods yard was closed and the Brampton branch cut back to just a short length serving the tube works.

In 1965 BR proposed the withdrawal of all remaining passenger services from the GC main line with the sections between Renishaw Central and Staveley, and Duckmanton and Kirkby Bentinck Colliery closing completely, claiming an annual saving of £1 million. A spur would connect Staveley Central to the Midland lines. And so in the early hours of 4th September 1966, after eight years of being deliberately run down, the last passenger train to run the full length of the GC main line completed its final journey. A single line from Killamarsh to Duckmanton North Junction was retained along with the curve up to Arkwright Town to serve Arkwright Colliery, the Staveley spur evidently not required. Chesterfield Central goods depot closed in September 1967.

The year 1969 saw all signalling south of the regional boundary at Horns Bridge brought under the control of the newly commissioned Trent Power Signal Box. Subsequent extensions to the Sheffield area resignalling and new Sheffield power box commissioned in 1973 would, eventually, come to embrace all surviving lines south to Chesterfield, making traditional signal boxes and semaphore signals a thing of the past.

Rail traffic at Ramcroft Colliery ended in 1966, Holmewood Colliery closed in 1968, Williamthorpe in 1970 and the Pilsley branch from Avenue Junction to Alma Junction was abandoned. The network remained fairly stable during the 1970s but rail traffic had ended at Ireland Colliery by 1976 and Glapwell Colliery had gone over to MGR operation, but the coal preparation plant closed within a year and the line from Seymour Junction was cut back to

Local passenger services were withdrawn from the Great Central main line and the Chesterfield Loop in March 1963. B1 4-6-0 No. 61166 pulls into Killamarsh Central on 30th June 1962 with a local service from Sheffield Victoria. *Tony Cooke/Colour-Rail*

Bolsover. The end of rail traffic at Sheepbridge works came shortly after its takeover by GKN in 1973.

The 1980s and 90s, as is well known, would be a different matter. What remained of the Sheepbridge branch closed along with the Wagon Repairs works it remained to serve, and Staveley iron works ceased using rail in 1985 after years of declining use. Arkwright Colliery traffic ended in 1988 and with it the last stretch of the GC main line in this area and the last remaining section of the Chesterfield Market Place line. Renishaw Park Colliery and its connection to the "Old Road" followed in 1989.

With declining traffic levels, Barrow Hill shed - Britain's last operating roundhouse - closed in February 1991 following the opening of a new train crew depot in Worksop and the transfer of maintenance to Shirebrook. Thanks to the hard work of the Barrow Hill Engine Shed Society with the support of local councils and other bodies it was preserved and today, while a working museum, it remains an operational base for several railway industry and heritage interests while being open to the public most weekends. Avenue Coking Plant and what remained of Avenue Sidings went in 1992, Markham Colliery - opened by the Staveley Coal & Iron Co. in the 1880s and the biggest pit in the area - closed in 1993, and Bolsover Colliery that same year.

Also in 1993 BR, incredibly, told Chesterfield Cylinders, the engineering firm relying on the last portion of the Brampton branch, that it didn't want their business anymore, despite traffic being on the increase. Meanwhile, the Oxcroft Junction-Clowne-Elmton & Creswell stretch of line had been quietly falling into disuse, disappearing beneath the undergrowth while the possibility of reintroducing a passenger service as an extension of the Nottingham-Worksop Robin Hood line revival was discussed in vain. Clay Cross works, the once huge coal and iron complex founded by George Stephenson and partners, much slimmed down, was closed in 2000 immediately after being taken over by the French company Saint Gobain.

At the start of the new millennium the Chesterfield area's rail network comprised the main line through Chesterfield to Sheffield via Dore & Totley, the "Old Road" northwards from Tapton Junction, the Hope Valley line, and branches from Barrow Hill via Seymour Junction to the Coalite works at Bolsover and Oxcroft Colliery - a surface extraction operation since closure of the mine in 1974. The Coalite plant closed in 2004 and Oxcroft in 2006 leaving us with the railway we have today - or at least at the time of writing.

Last outpost of BR steam. Williamthorpe Colliery, Heath, is remembered for being the last working place for BR's "Jinties" - the Class 3F 0-6-0 tanks which were hired to the National Coal Board from Westhouses depot. At 11.45am on Saturday 16th October 1965, No. 47611 shunts 47535 prior to all fires being dropped for the weekend. *Robert Anderson*

THE MIDLAND: CLAY CROSS TO KILLAMARSH & BRANCHES

ABOVE: The point where the North Midland main line enters this volume of Railway Memories. En-route from Derby it has just emerged from Clay Cross Tunnel and is passing underneath the short branch leading from alongside Clay Cross station up to the iron works and, until closure in 1963, the Town goods depot. This view is dated Saturday 10th June 1978. The small building with the hipped roof is a weighbridge house. The furnaces are visible in the left distance.
BELOW: From the above scene the works branch curved round into the Clay Cross foundry as seen here on the same day. The lean-to garage on the right is the foundry's standard gauge engine shed. *Both Adrian Booth*

Clay Cross private sidings 1956: Clay Cross Co.'s iron works; Derbyshire Carriage & Wagon Co. Ltd.; Doncaster Wagon Co. Ltd.; East Midlands Gas Board(via Clay Cross Co.'s siding.) Prior to this there had also been a brickworks siding(situated between the Town goods yard and the iron works,) and Clay Cross No.7(Danesmoor) Colliery, connected to the Erewash Valley line, which had gone since 1938. In the 19th Century there had been an engine shed situated on the east side of the station which was later converted and expanded into the wagon repair shops.

ABOVE: Clay Cross station looking north shortly before closure as a two-car Derby Works DMU calls, bound for the city where it was built. Lines leading up to Clay Cross Town goods yard and the iron works are over on the far left. *Railway Station Photographs*

BELOW: The chalet-style station buildings on the road overbridge at Clay Cross on Monday 17th April 1967, three months after closure. Given that the station was a mile and a half from the town, closure seemed inevitable. *Ray Woodmore collection*

Goods facilities at Clay Cross station were listed in the 1956 Railway Clearing House Handbook of Stations as being equipped to handle general goods, livestock and horse boxes and carriage trucks with a 4-ton capacity crane. The Town goods yard was equipped with a 11/2-ton crane and able to handle general goods only.

The station closed to goods on 4th May 1964 and to passengers from 2nd January 1967. The Town goods yard was closed from 7th October 1963.

In summer 1961 between 6.34am and 10.56pm, *30 passenger trains called at Clay Cross station each weekday: 10 Down and seven Up on the Nottingham line, and five Down and eight Up on the Derby line. Most were Sheffield-Nottingham or Derby local services with one or two running just between Clay Cross and Chesterfield or Sheffield. Extra trains called on Saturdays, including the 7.25am Nottingham-Blackpool; 8.20am Great Yarmouth-Sheffield; 3.10pm from Skegness which was advertised to terminate at Clay Cross at 7.10pm; the 7.35am Sheffield-Skegness and the 9.33am Blackpool-Nottingham. No trains called there on Sundays.*

Clay Cross wagon shops and sidings 1964. *Not to scale*

Strathfield Colliery
Former Springfield Brickworks
Former line to Clay Cross No.4 Colliery
Station Road
Doncaster Wagon Works
Level crossing
Traverser
Traverser
Station
Cattle dock
Derbyshire Carriage & Wagon Co.
Signal box
From Leeds
To Trent Jn.
To Clay Cross Foundry and Town goods yard
To Derby
©Stephen Chapman 2019

BELOW: Since closing, the wagon shops at Clay Cross have been used for storing various items on behalf of the Tramway Museum Society, Crich. This lucky shot from a passing train on Wednesday 13th May 1964 shows tramcar No. 14 from BR's Grimsby & Immingham tramway. It is outside the Derbyshire Carriage & Wagon Co. shops which, according to 19th Century Ordnance Survey plans, had originally been a 6-road engine shed. *Stephen Chapman archive*

HASLAND SIDINGS TO TAPTON JUNCTION

BRITISH RAILWAYS EASTERN REGION(SOUTHERN AREA) SECTIONAL APPENDIX 1969

SIGNALLING: Absolute block on Up and Down Main Lines. Permissive Block on Up and Down Goods lines.

MAXIMUM SPEED: On Main Lines: 80mph **On Goods Lines:** 45mph

LOOPS AND REFUGE SIDINGS: Down Refuge Siding at Horns Bridge with standage for 31 wagons, engine & brake van; Down Goods Loop at Tapton Junction with standage for 57 wagons, engine & brake van.

SIGNAL BOXES(with distance from previous box): Avenue Crossing(1346yds from Clay Cross North Jn.;)Hasland Sidings; Horns Bridge(1 mile 907yds from Hasland Sidings;) Chesterfield South(807yds;) Tapton Jn.(1221yds.)

The LMS 1935 Sectional Appendix shows a second Goods Line Clay Cross South Jn.-North Jn.

ABOVE: Ex-Midland Railway 4F 0-6-0 No. 43953 heads south past Avenue Sidings at Wingerworth with the returning 1X20 Midland Requiem railtour on Saturday 16th October 1965. The Avenue coking plant sidings are on the left. *Mike Mitchell/Transport Treasury*

Opened in 1875 Hasland motive power depot was coded 18C subordinate to Toton until 1963 when it became 16H in the Nottingham Division. Although mainly a freight shed, it also had a small stud of passenger engines for local services, including those between Chesterfield and Rotherham Westgate. The shed closed in September 1964. The passenger allocation included 2P 4-4-0 No. 40337 seen(above) alongside sister 40502 inside the roofless roundhouse on Sunday 11th September 1955. Notice how the wall needs extra support, possibly due to subsidence or instability following removal of the roof. *Neville Stead collection/Transport Library*

Locomotives allocated to Hasland as per 21st May 1955:
2P 4-4-0: 40337/402/18/91/502/37/50/6/7; Deeley 0F 0-4-0T: 41531; Johnson 3F 0-6-0: 43211/2; Fowler Midland 4F 0-6-0: 43891/959; Fowler LMS 4F 0-6-0: 44053/4/136/62/244/88/94/410/603; Ivatt 2MT 2-6-0: 46499/500; Kitson LMS 0-4-0ST: 47003/4; LMS 3F 0-6-0T: 47272/8/423; Fowler LMS Beyer-Garratt 2-6-6-2T: 47968/73/7/8/80/2/3/6/92/3/7; 8F 2-8-0: 48065/95/371; Johnson 2F 0-6-0: 58153/76. Total 46.

Summer 1964: Fowler Midland 4F 0-6-0: 43967/82; Fowler LMS 4F 0-6-0: 44054/381/463/603; LMS 3F 0-6-0T: 47272/423/535/43/611; 8F 2-8-0: 48116/87/205/359/71/495/547; 350hp diesel electric 0-6-0: D3792. Total 19.
Depot closed from 9th September.

Hasland shunting duties 1956:
No.47 Class 3 tank engine to shunt Clay Cross and Stretton 6.15am Monday to 5am Sunday.
No. 48 Class 3 tank engine to shunt 24hr daily 10.45pm-10.45pm (start 6am Mondays, finish 6am Saturday) at Avenue Sidings, engine working alternate days with target 149. Nos. 49 and 50 were spare.

Hasland Trip duties: In 1956, when it came under the Rotherham District Operating Superintendent, Hasland provided power for six trip diagrams:
Target 144 left Avenue Sidings at 7.20am and made repeated return trips to Grassmoor and Alma Junction until finishing at Avenue Sidings at 4.20pm.
Target 145 worked 6.55am to 3.35pm daily to and from Alma Junction serving Grassmoor and Holmewood collieries and shunting Avenue Sidings from 9.20 to 11.35am.
On Mondays **Target 146** began by leaving Hasland shed light engine at 5.30am for Dunston & Barlow, returning to Clay Cross by 8.40 and then to Danesmoor by 9.20 where it was booked to shunt. It then worked repeated trips between Danesmoor, Clay Cross and Avenue. On other weekdays it left Hasland shed light engine at 8.30am for Danesmoor where it took up the same workings as Monday, finishing at Avenue Sidings at 9.12pm, earlier on Saturdays.
Target 147 worked 7.45am to 9.55pm daily and ran Avenue-Chesterfield North Sidings-Dronfield CS-Chesterfield Yard(where it was booked to "shunt and prepare train")-Hollis Lane-Avenue-Clay Cross-Tibshelf Goods-Stoneyford Junction where it was booked to shunt, then to Codnor Park-Clay Cross-Avenue.
Target 148 worked 8am to 7.38pm daily. It ran light engine to Seymour Jn. then returned via Avenue Sidings to Grassmor Colliery, returning to Avenue by 11.50 am where it was booked to work trips and shunt as required, including servicing Avenue Coke Plant. It then ran to Staveley Down Sidings, returning to Clay Cross via a 50-minute spell at Dunston & Barlow, then light to Hasland shed.
Target 149 left Hasland shed light engine at 7.30am for Chesterfield where it made trips to and from Brampton, the gas works and Hollis Lane before returning light to Hasland shed.
All workings were specified "Class 4 Freight Engine" except 149 which was "Class 3 Tank Engine."
By 1963 trip workings were being issued on a weekly basis by the Divisional Manager, Nottingham.

Between 1955 and 1958 the Garratts were shared between Toton and Hasland with Toton having the majority. No. 47982 sits by the water tower at Hasland shed on Sunday 11th September 1955. The dereliction of the roundhouse exemplifies the appaling working conditions which many steam shed staff had to tolerate in later years. *Neville Stead collection/Transport Library*

Hasland to Doe Hill(Pilsley Road Crossing) was shown in the LMS 1935 Sectional Appendix as being worked by Token between Avenue Sidings and Grassmoor East and by Train Staff between Grassmoor East and Williamthorpe level crossing, and also between Pilsley Road Crossing and Morton Sidings.
Avenue Crossing to Avenue Sidings signal box was worked as "Goods yard."
Mileages were: Avenue Crossing-Avenue Sidings: 708yds; Avenue Sidings-Grassmoor Jn.: 572yds; Grassmoor Jn.-East: 1 mile 198yds; Grassmoor East-Lings Colliery Sidings: 1540yds: Williamthorpe Level Crossing-Pilsley Road Crossing 2 miles 1248yds; Pilsley Road Level Crossing-Morton Sidings: 1 mile 198yds. Grassmoor East was the only intermediate block post/token station between Hasland and Pilsley.
The Appendix also states: The line from **Grassmoor Jn. to Grassmoor Sidings and Bond's Main Colliery (LNER)** is worked by token. The Up direction is from Grassmoor Jn. to Bond's Main Colliery(LNE.) Trains were restricted to 15mph.

LEFT: Holmewood Colliery was served by a single track branch of approximately 1100 yards which left the Pilsley-Grassmoor-Hasland line at Holmewood Jn. on Stainsby Common, just north of Pilsley alongside the GC main line. This view looking north east from the B6039 Tibshelf Road on Saturday 8th October 1966 shows the line's approach to the colliery. The colliery was also connected to the GC main line at Heath station sidings and south of Heath. The girder bridge carries the GC main line.
Mike Mitchell/Transport Treasury

Grassmoor Branch. "The single line between a point opposite the 143 1/2 milepost in Avenue Sidings and Grassmoor East is worked by token with "No Signalman" type of token instruments at Avenue Sidings, and no train must proceed on to the single line between Avenue Sidings and Grassmoor East unless the driver is in possession of a token, or he has been shown the token which has been delivered to the driver of an engine to which his engine is attached.......Auxiliary Key token instruments are provided at Grassmoor Junction and Grassmoor Colliery Sidings Nos. 1 and 2 ground frames and guards or shunters with trains having to do work at these places or be shunted clear inside for other trains to pass will require to use these instruments in accordance with the instructions exhibited at these places. The fireman will be similarly responsible in the case of a light engine....The person working the instrument at Avenue Sidings must be regarded as the signalman.
A special token instrument is provided at the Grassmoor Junction stage in which the token for the Grassmoor branch carried by trains for Bond's Main Colliery must be placed by the shunter, to enable trains to work through between Avenue Sidings and Grassmoor East signal box during the time the train is on the Bond's Main branch. The connection between the Grassmoor Branch and the Bond's Main Colliery branch is worked from a stage and controlled by the tokens for the Grassmoor Junction and Bond's Main Signal Colliery Sidings section as well as those for the Avenue Sidings and Grassmoor East section....The driver working a train to Bond's Main Colliery must not on arrival at that place hand the token to the signalman, but must retain it in his possession until he returns to Grassmoor Junction, when he must hand it to the shunter there." *LMS 1935 Sectional Appendix*

"In order that more than one train may be between **Grassmoor East Box and Holmewood Colliery** or the scotch block near Bridge No. 2, half a mile on the Holmewood side of Pilsley at the same time, the line...is, when necessary, worked by pilot guard, without tickets, in accordance with the regulations for working single lines of railway by pilot guard. The pilot guard will have possession of the Staff which will be shown to each driver. The pilot guard will...despatch a train from Grassmoor East to Holmewood Colliery or scotch block near Bridge No.2..but must in all cases accompany the following train as far as it requires to proceed. The pilot guard must remain with the second train until despatched from Ling's Colliery sidings for Grassmoor East signal box...after the pilot guard has despatched the subsequent train from Ling's Colliery sidings he must then walk to Holmewood Junction and accompany the other train from [there] to Grassmoor East signal box. Not more than two trains may be between Grassmoor East....and Holmewood Junction or scotch block...at one time except that when a second train has been assisted by a bank engine in the rear...." *LMS Sectional Appendix 1935*

ABOVE: Williamthorpe Colliery was connected to the Hasland-Pilsley line by a short branch from Alma and Lings Colliery junctions consisting of two lines becoming three. One led from the outward sidings, another to the inward sidings and a third by-passed the colliery sidings, passed under the GC main line and curved south to join the GC at Heath station sidings. BR "Jinty" 3F 0-6-0T No. 47383 blasts through the yard and past the colliery screens with a rake of internal NCB wagons on Thursday 1st June 1967. *Adrian Booth*

BELOW: Following release from the Cromford & High Peak line, BR's last working J94 0-6-0ST, No. 68012, was also sent by Westhouses to work at Williamthorpe Colliery. Here on Saturday 24th June 1967, it takes refreshment from an old Lancashire boiler which has conveniently made an excellent water tank. No. 68012 was withdrawn in October 1967 and sent to South Wales for scrap early in 1968. The line which by-passed the colliery and continued to the GC main line at Heath is on the far left. *Adrian Booth*

ABOVE: One of Hasland's ex-LMS 4F 0-6-0s, No.44054, approaches Horns Bridge, south of Chesterfield Midland station, with the 7.55am Toton to Canklow empties at 9.53am on Saturday 5th October 1963. *Robert Anderson*

BELOW: Breakdown crane required at Horns Bridge 1. Class 8F 2-8-0 No. 48694 has come to grief on the points at Horns Bridge requiring the aid of a breakdown crane which had been brought by a Brush Type 2 diesel(Class 31.) The derailment has blocked both the Up Main and Down Goods lines. On the right, a Stanier Class 5 4-6-0 gingerly threads its way by on the Up Goods with a stopping passenger train. Notice the old and new signal boxes, the elder on the left listing the opposite way to the spire. *Tom Greaves*

ABOVE: Breakdown crane required at Horns Bridge 11. Two 45-ton steam cranes - one from Healey Mills, West Yorkshire - are engaged in bridge work at Horns Bridge on Sunday 15th August 1976 as a Sulzer Type 4 "Peak" passes with an unidentified Up express. The background is filled with Markham's engineering works where internal wagons can be seen just beyond the nearest crane. The "Peak" appears to be right over the former Chesterfield Loop while the view is almost certainly from the abandoned LD&EC line. *Robert Anderson*

RIGHT: Ruston & Hornsby 4-wheel diesel mechanical loco No. 476141 built in 1963 was used by Markham & Co. to shunt their internal rail system. It is seen here on 9th April 1980. *Adrian Booth*

Private Sidings listed in the 1956 Handbook of Stations as being at or near Chesterfield Midland: Chesterfield Tube Co. Ltd.; British Furnaces Ltd., via Chesterfield Tube Co.; Bryan, Donkin & Co., via Chesterfield Tube Co.; Clayton's Tannery(makers of bridles and brief cases etc.;) Eastwood's Wagon Works; Markham & Co. Broad Oaks Iron Works; Robinson & Sons Ltd. Portland Works; Saunders Brick Works, Storforth Lane Siding; Steel Breaking & Dismantling Co. Ltd., Lockoford Siding; Chesterfield Corporation Siding; Chesterfield & District Co-op Society Ltd., Siding. There was also Lord's Mill Wharf which closed in August 1953.

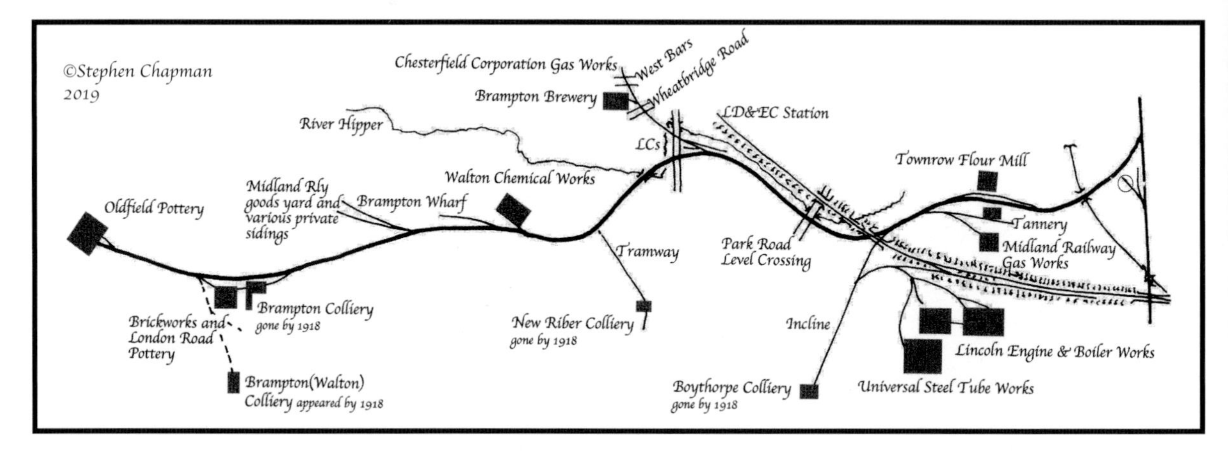

ABOVE: The Brampton goods branch(also known as the Boythorpe Wharf branch) and its various connections c1900.

BELOW: This tube works ensured survival of what remained of the Brampton branch until the late 1990s. At the time of this photo on Wednesday 9th April 1980 the works was under the management of Tube Investments Ltd. and rail traffic within the works was shunted by this 4-wheel diesel built by Thomas Hill of Kilnhurst in 1966, builder's No. 166v. *Adrian Booth*

The 1½-mile Brampton Branch was shown by the LMS 1935 Sectional Appendix as single line worked according to One Engine in Steam(or two or more engines coupled together) rules. The Staff permitting a train to enter the line was round, black and retained at Horns Bridge signal box. The regular Brampton branch pilot in 1963 was Hasland Trip 19 which ran light engine from Hasland shed to Chesterfield, arriving 12.48pm, departing Hollis Lane for Hasland at 8.30pm and specified "steam engine;"

Brampton goods yard, listed in the 1938 Handbook of Stations as Brampton Wharf, was shown as equipped to handle general goods traffic with a 1 ton 15cwt permanent crane. It also listed Boythorpe Lane Wharf as equipped to handle general goods with no crane. In the 1956 Handbook only Boythorpe Lane Wharf was listed. It was closed from 15th June 1964. An engine siding and 55ft turntable were situated at Brampton Branch Junction, in the fork between the branch and the main line.

Brampton Branch private sidings 1938: Brampton Brewery Co.; British Furnaces Ltd.,(access via Chesterfield Tube Co.;) Bryan, Donkin & Co. and Chesterfield Tube Co.(joint access;) Chesterfield Corporation Electric Lighting Depot; Chesterfield Corporation Gas Works Siding; Chesterfield Corporation Siding(via Pearson's;) Chesterfield District Co-op Society; Midland Rly. Co.'s Gas Works; J. Pearson's London & Oldfield Potteries; Plowright Bros. Engineers Siding; Robinson & Sons Pharmaceuticals Ltd., Goyt Siding(via Pearson's;) Sheffield Pure Ice & Cold Storage Co.; Shellmex & BP Ltd.; T. Townrow's Flour Mill Siding; J. S. Wilcockson Siding.

ABOVE: A portion of the Brampton goods branch in around 1950. The overgrown sidings in the foreground once led to the Midland Railway's gas works and a tannery as well as forming a headshunt for the tube works. Lords Mill Street is on the extreme right while the large old building is T. Townrow's flour mill. *Stephen Chapman archive*

BELOW: The end of the line for the Brampton branch. Looking outwards from the tube works sidings towards the former connections with the Brampton Branch and the main line in 1998 shortly after rail traffic had ended. The LD&EC line from Market Place station used to pass over roughly where the nearest trees are. The erstwhile flour mill in the picture above can be seen above the tree on the right. The car park is roughly on the course of the incline to long-closed Boythorpe Colliery. *From a colour negative by Stephen Chapman*

Pictures of the Brampton branch are extremely rare, and only those shown here have come to light during searches for this book. Did no-one ever photograph the "Jinty" working the line, shunting Boythorpe Wharf or at Park Road level crossing? If anyone out there did, Bellcode Books would love to hear from you and would be delighted to publish your photo in a forthcoming Railway Memories.

ABOVE: With Hollis Lane sidings on the right, Hasland's 2P 4-4-0 No. 40409 sets off southbound from Chesterfield Midland with a stopping passenger train on Thursday 23rd April 1953.
R.E.Vincent/Transport Treasury

CENTRE: Chesterfield Midland's impressive goods offices and warehouse stand empty and gaunt against a forboding sky in 1998. *From a colour slide by Stephen Chapman*
Chesterfield Midland was listed in 1956 as able to handle all classes of freight and equipped with a 5-ton capacity permanent crane(10-ton in 1938.) There was a second goods shed off the picture to the left as can be seen in the pictiure on page 19. Goods facilities survived into the 1980s but by the time of the above picture all track had been lifted save for a couple of sidings for enginers' use and shunting the tube works.

LEFT: Chesterfield Midland station exterior draped in Union flags ready to be unfurled, so maybe a Royal visit is awaited or perhaps it is Coronation time in 1953.
Railway Station Photographs

ABOVE: The p. way gang look on as Normanton-allocated 3F 0-6-0 No. 43321 passes by Chesterfield Midland with an Up Through Freight on Thursday 5th September 1957. The station's 1870 buildings are clearly visible in the background. *Peter Hay/Transport Library*

BELOW: Another of Hasland's 2P 4-4-0s, No. 40556, is given the road from Chesterfield Midland while working an Up stopping passenger service. The station - 146¼ miles from St. Pancras - consisted of two through platforms plus an Up bay platform at the south end and a Down bay at the north end. The bays were removed during rebuilding in the 1960s but in recent times an additional through platform has been established on the former Down Goods line. *Peter Cookson*

Chesterfield Midland. Down Passenger Trains Starting from Up PLatform. When necessary, a Down passenger train may be started from the Up platform under the supervision of the Station Master, who will be responsible for seeing that all points which become facing points are securely clipped and locked for the passage of each train from the Up line platform to the Down line. *LMS Sectional Appendix 1935*

ABOVE: Viewed from the diesel loco cab of a Down passenger train at Chesterfield Midland, WD 2-8-0 No. 90189 heads a class 7 train of empties southbound along the Up Main on Friday 10th April 1964. Eastwood's wagon works on the left had by this time become a scrap yard. *Roy Wood/Peter Rose collection*

BELOW: Stanier 8F 2-8-0 No. 48772 darkens the heavens as it heads south along the "Old Road" at Tapton Junction with an Up class 8 freight at 1.40pm on 5th October 1963. This is the junction between the "Old Road" and the Sheffield line(the two running lines on the left) but the two routes run alongside each other for about half a mile before parting company. *Robert Anderson*

ABOVE: "Hey look at these.." exclaims Leeds Holbeck driver Arthur Suttill from the cab of Jubilee 4-6-0 No. 45570 *New Zealand* while working what is thought to be the summer Saturday 6.50 am Paignton-Bradford in the early 1960s. The old London tube trains are waiting to be cut up at the Lockoford yard of Steel Breaking & Dismantling just north of Tapton Junction. The picture is unfortunately undated but No. 45570 was one of the Class 6P and 7P locos reallocated to Sheffield Darnall following the closure of Millhouse shed in 1962. The scrap yard with the tube stock is also visible on the far left of the previous picture. *Peter Rose*

RIGHT: Not everything that goes into a scrapyard is broken up. The cab of ex-BR Drewry diesel shunter D2218 proved to be a very useful addition to the yard crane at Steel Breaking & Dismantling, as seen on Monday 20th July 1970.
From a colour slide by Adrian Booth

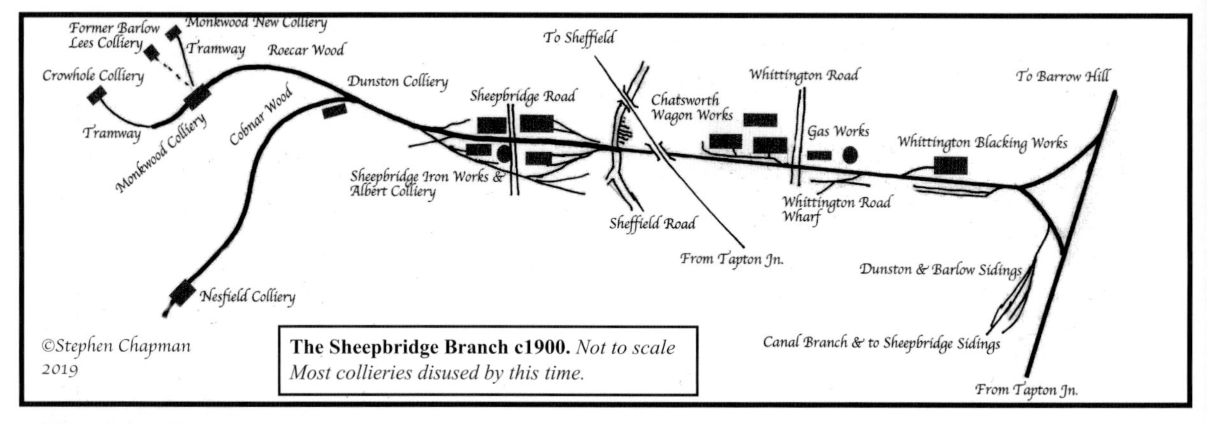

The Sheepbridge Branch c1900. *Not to scale Most collieries disused by this time.*

The 1935 LMS Sectional Appendix described the lines between **Dunston & Barlow Sidings, the Canal branch and Sheepbridge Lane level crossing** as worked by One Engine in Steam regulations using a square blue Staff retained at Sheffield Road crossing. The shunter or signalman at Dunston & Barlow South was the person authorized to deliver the Staff to or receive it from the driver.

The 1935 LMS Sectional Appendix showed the line from **Sheepbridge Lane level crossing to Nesfield and Monkswood** as worked by "One Engine in Steam" regulations using a round, black Staff retained at Sheepbridge Lane level crossing, the crossing keeper being the person authorized to deliver the Staff to or receive it from the driver.

The Nesfield Colliery branch described as: "Stage. Controlled by Staff key."

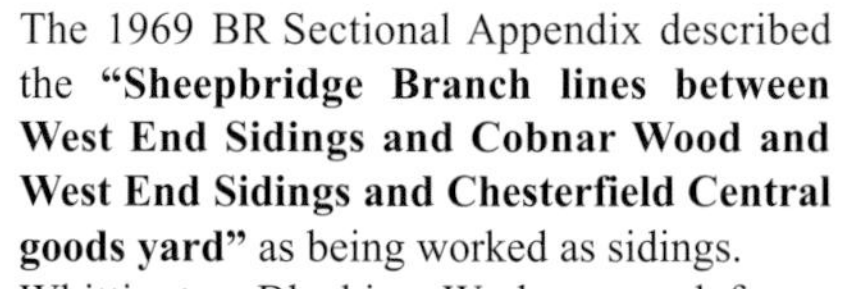

The 1969 BR Sectional Appendix described the **"Sheepbridge Branch lines between West End Sidings and Cobnar Wood and West End Sidings and Chesterfield Central goods yard"** as being worked as sidings.

Whittington Blacking Works ground frame "released by Annett's key 'A' kept in West End Sidings shunter's cabin.

Wagon Repairs ground frame "released by Annett's key 'C' kept at Whittington Road Crossing."

Cobnar Wood ground frame: "The key to the door of the frame is kept in Sheffield Road yard shunter's cabin."

The two pictures on this page are scenes from the Wagon Repairs Chatsworth works on Saturday 10th June 1978 - the last surviving business on the Sheepbridge branch. Above is the overhead electric traverser used to moved wagons between various shops while, left, this, believe it or not, is a works shunter. An actual locomotive from the earliest days of diesel, it was built by Bagulay of Burton-on-Trent in 1934, builders' No. 2082. There was also a Ruston & Hornsby diesel. *Both Adrian Booth*

In steam days, the Sheepbridge Coal & Iron Co. had a considerable and varied fleet of locomotives at its Sheepbridge works. There would have been more at its ironstone quarries in North Lincolnshire and Northamptonshire, and at its Langwith Colliery.
RIGHT: Here we have No.21, an 0-6-0ST built by Hudswell, Clarke & Co. of Leeds in 1883, works No. 248 as proclaimed on the rectangular brass plate on the cabside. The plate above it reads "Rebuilt by the Sheepbridge Company." No. 21 is seen in front of the large slag heap by the site of Albert Colliery. *Neville Stead Collection/Transport Library*

LEFT: At work with BR wagons deep inside the Sheepbridge iron works on Sunday 5th March 1961 is No. 23, also a Hudswell, Clarke 0-6-0ST. Despite surroundings of smoke and grime, the driver is dressed in Sunday Best collar and tie. The Sheepbridge company was bought by the Staveley Iron Co. in 1955 and later became part of GKN.
R.C.Riley/Transport Treasury

Right: On the same day is seen the powerful looking No. 26, built by Avonside of Bristol in 1929, works No. 1825.
R.C.Riley/Transport Treasury

LMS and BR locos were also stabled at Sheepbridge which was regarded as a "sub-shed" of Barrow Hill. A shed for works engines was situated in the centre of the works.
By 1973 just one locomotive remained at Sheepbridge, by then just Sheepbridge Rolling Mills Ltd. The engine was a Thomas Hill 0-4-0 diesel hydraulic, works No. 116c, rebuilt in 1962 from a 1945-built Fowler locomotive.

***The former Midland Railway Sheepbridge Branch** left the "Old Road" at the 1473/4 milepost(from St. Pancras.) The junction between the Monkswood and Nesfield branches was situated west of the iron works, mid-way between 1491/4 and 1491/2 mileposts. By 1964 what remained of the Monkswood branch terminated at 150 milepost, alongside Roecar Wood reservoir. The Nesfield branch by this time continued a short distance to a point just beyond Cobnar Wood, short of the coal loading point it had once served.*

Sheepbridge Yard. The single-armed signal near the Sheepbridge Co.'s fitting shop is used to regulate the running of trains from the Sheepbridge Co.'s ironworks sidings, between the fitting shop and the stores, on to the incline sidings leading to Sheffield Road.

The signal is worked by guards and shunters by means of a turnover lever near the connections leading from the incline sidings to the cinder tip and furnace lines and must be kept at the "Clear" position, except when required to be placed at "Danger" for the protection of LMS engines proceeding towards the fitting shop or crossing the incline sidings when passing between the cinder tip lines and furnace lines. During the time this signal is at "Danger" no vehicle from the Sheepbridge Co.'s sidings....must be placed on either side of the incline sidings leading to Sheffield Road.

The single-armed signal fixed alongside the incline siding, giving permission for LMS engines to proceed to the Bank Sidings must be left in the "Danger" position, except when required to be taken off for LMS engines to pass. The signal must be taken off by the LMS guard or shunter who must, before taking it off, place the signal applicable to the Sheepbridge Co.'s engines leaving the Furnace Cutting sidings to "Danger."....

As soon as the LMS engine has passed, the signal applicable to the incline siding must be placed to "Danger." The signal applicable to the Furnace Cutting Sidings must be left in the "Danger" position, and when the LMS engine has returned from the Bank sidings to the Sheepbridge branch it will be taken off when necessary by the Sheepbridge Co.'s men. *LMS Section Appendix 1935*

Sheepbridge Private Sidings 1938. Nesfield branch: Booker & Sons.; Pearson & Co. Sheepbridge Branch: Borough of Chesterfield Highway Dept. Pottery Lane Siding; W. Prestwich & Sons Cinder Breaker Siding; Sheepbridge Coal & Iron Co. Iron Works; Sheepbridge Coal & Iron Co. New Pipe Works; Sheepbridge Gas Works; Sheepbridge Stokes Centrifugal Casting Co.(via iron works;) Wagon Repairs Ltd.; W. Cumming & Co., Whittington Blacking Works; Pearson & Co. Whittington Moor Potteries. There was also a public goods siding known as Whittington Road Public Wharf.

Short sections of the Nesfield and Monkswood branches continued to serve slag tips and opencast coal workings around Cobnar Wood into the 1960s.

Again on Sunday 5th March 1961, 0-6-0ST Sheepbridge No. 28 has charge of slag ladels at the west end of the works.
R.C.Riley/Transport Treasury

Looking north along the "Old Road" at Whittington station and signal box. The picture is undated but a lack of station nameboards and shelters suggest it is some time after closure which occurred with effect from 4th February 1952. There were no goods facilities at Whittington station. The private siding passing through the gate led to an engineering works but at one time it continued as an industrial tramway to West Staveley and Hundall collieries. A separate tramway came down from numerous small coal pits around Hundall to Dixon's Wharf on the Chesterfield Canal, passing along the backs of houses in New Whittington, and under the siding and station on the way. By 1898 the tramways and collieries were all gone. Barrow Hill Down Sidings signal box is just visible in the distance.
Railway Station Photographs

TAPTON JUNCTION TO KILLAMARSH

BRITISH RAILWAYS EASTERN REGION SECTIONAL APPENDIX 1960

SIGNALLING: Absolute block on Up and Down Main Lines. Permissive Block on Up and Down Goods lines.

MAXIMUM SPEED: On Main Lines: 60mph **On Goods Lines:** 45mph

UP & DOWN GOODS LINES: Whittington-Barrow Hill Jn.; Foxlow Jn.-Renishaw Park Goods Jn.
Up Goods Barrow Hill South-Junction worked in both directions.

LOOPS AND REFUGE SIDINGS: Down Refuge Siding at Dunston & Barlow with standage for 39 wagons, engine & brake van and Up Refuge Siding with standage for 31 wagons, engine & brake van; Down Refuge Siding at Foxlow Junction with standage for 40 wagons, engine & brake van; Holbrook Colliery Sidings: Up Refuge Siding with standage for 78 wagons, engine & brake van; Down Refuge Siding at Killamarsh Branch Sidings with standage for 44 wagons, engine & brake van.

SIGNAL BOXES(with distance from previous box): Dunston & Barlow South(1034yds from Tapton Jn.;) Dunston & Barlow North(642yds;) Whittington(1mile 77yds.;) Barrow Hill Down Sidings(352yds. Block post on Goods lines only;) Barrow Hill Up Sidings(410yds. Block post on Goods lines only;) Barrow Hill South(918yds from Whittington;) Barrow Hill Jn.(450yds.;) Foxlow Jn.(1546yds.;) Renishaw Park Goods Jn.(1mile 273yds.;)Eckington(1306yds.:) Holbrook Colliery Sidings(1mile 937yds.;) Killamarsh West Station(627yds.;)Killamarsh Branch Sidings(671yds;) Beighton Jn.(1623yds.)

The LMS 1935 Sectional Appendix described the Barrow Hill signal boxes as "Staveley." Signal boxes at Dunston & Barlow South, Barrow Hill Down Sidings, Holbrook Colliery Sidings and Killamarsh Branch Sidings had been eliminated by the time of the 1969 Sectional Appendix.

ABOVE: Barrow Hill was the centre of freight operations on the Midland lines in North Derbyshire with its yards and motive power depot, and remained so until the final demise of the coal industry in the 1990s. In fact there was once a control office at Staveley which was open six days a week. On one of the occasions when the "Old Road" was required as a diversionary route between Sheffield and Chesterfield, BR/Sulzer "Peak" Type 4 No. 45105 charges south through a fine array of semaphore signals at the head of an Up express on Tuesday 25th March 1975. Barrow Hill Down Sidings are on the left and the Up sidings behind the train.
From a Colour-Rail slide by I.Hayward

BELOW: Stanier 8F 2-8-0 No. 48547 trundles its considerable load of freight along the Down Main with Barrow Hil Up and Down sidings on each side at 12.50pm on Saturday 6th October 1962. The former Springwell branch leading to Barrow Hill engine shed can just be glimpsed beyond 48547's front end. This branch, described as Staveley South to Engine Shed in the 1935 Sectional Appendix, was not worked by any block or bell signalling and drivers were instructed to run at slow speed and be prepared to stop short of any obstruction. The Down Goods line, which is behind the train, was subsequently lifted and deleted from the Sectional Appendix per a supplement issued on 5th April 1980. *Robert Anderson*

STAVELEY BARROW HILL engine shed is among the most historically significant in the country and today is the last working roundhouse. Situated just off the "Old Road" and connected to the Springwell branch, it was opened by the Midland Railway in 1870 and was coded 18D subordinate to Toton under the LMS and British Railways London Midland Region. The 1958, boundary changes saw it come under the Sheffield Division of the Eastern Region and it was then coded 41E until the mid-1970s when it was recoded BH. Barrow Hill was mainly a freight depot and provided engines for both longer distance and local main line freight work, trip duties and shunting, including engines for shunting at Staveley iron works under a hundred-year agreement made when the shed opened. Among enthusiasts it became especially notable for its allocation of veteran 0-4-0 and 0-6-0 tank engines retained largely for the Staveley works duties. Diesel facilities were commissioned in April 1965 when Barrow Hill received an allocation of the short-lived Clayton Type 1s, for which it also became notable. Barrow Hill closed to steam in October 1965, its allocation including the "Staveley tanks" going, on paper, to Langwith Junction but it continued to supply diesel shunters for the iron works. Barrow Hill had lost its own allocation of main line locomotives(Class 20s) by 1974 when it became a signing on point and outbase for locomotives from Tinsley, and latterly from Toton. It closed as a British Rail depot in 1991 following the opening of a new traincrew depot and stabling point at Worksop. Barrow Hill was of course reborn and is still with us as a working museum and a base for certain railway industry and heritage businesses, including the Deltic Preservation Society.

ABOVE: A classic 1960s Barrow Hill roundhouse scene c1965. Clayton Type 1 and Brush Type 2 diesels surround the turntable on which stands ex-Midland 1F 0-6-0T No. 41835 which had just been withdrawn from service. *Tom Greaves*

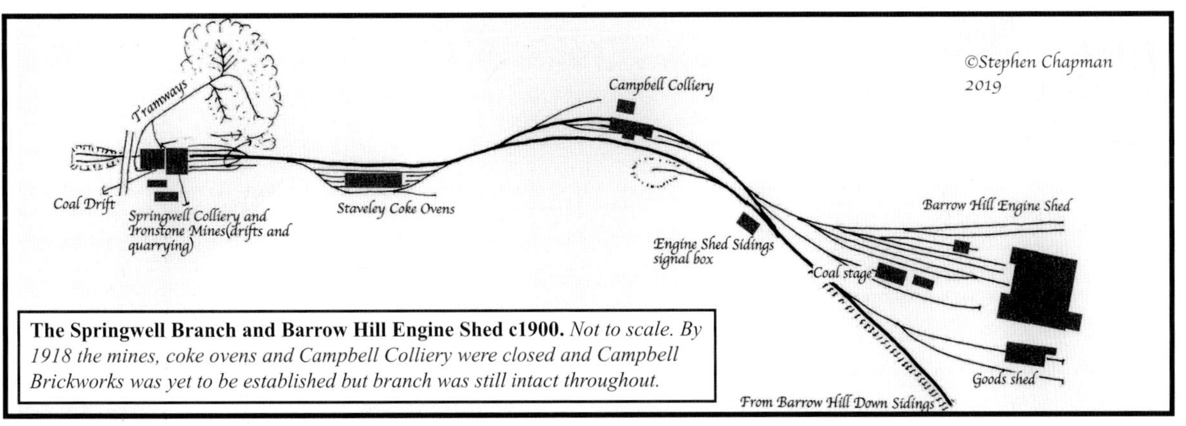

The Springwell Branch and Barrow Hill Engine Shed c1900. *Not to scale. By 1918 the mines, coke ovens and Campbell Colliery were closed and Campbell Brickworks was yet to be established but branch was still intact throughout.*

The Springwell branch was worked according to One Engine in Steam regulations with the use of a round, black Staff retained at Engine Shed Sidings signal box. The signalman there was the person authorized to deliver to and receive the Staff from the driver. By the 1930s the Springwell branch served only the Staveley Iron Company's Campbell Brickworks alongside the engine shed. Nowadays, a short portion is used as a demonstration line and shunting neck.

ABOVE: A trio of Barrow Hill's tanks sit a little uneasily next Clayton incomer No. D8605. The tanks are, from left: Kitson 0F 0-4-0ST No. 47001, 0F 0-4-0T No. 41533 and 1F 0-6-0T No. 41835. When Barrow Hill closed to steam in 1965 and Staveley Works shunting was turned over to diesels, the tanks were technically transferred to Langwith Junction but with that shed closing soon they went into store at Canklow instead. They finally ended up stored at Rotherham to await scrapping except for 41708 which was thankfully preserved.
Tom Greaves

LEFT: The steamy atmosphere of a roundhouse - but not gloomy for Barrow Hill has a well glazed roof letting in ample daylight. WD 2-8-0 No. 90688 sizzles peacefully next to Clayton No. D8612.
Tom Greaves

Locomotives allocated to 18D Barrow Hill as per 21st May 1955. Johnson Midland 0F 0-4-0ST: 41518; Deeley Midland 0F 0-4-0T: 41528/9/33/4; Johnson Midland 1F 0-6-0T: 41708/39/49/52/63/77/803/4; Johnson Midland 3F 0-6-0: 43224/34/98/310/86/515/24/46/75/605; Fowler Midland 4F 0-6-0: 43857/63/86/900/20/93/4010; Fowler LMS 4F 0-6-0:44066/70/104/22/9/47/249/67/99/371/404/75/590/606; LMS 3F 0-6-0T: 47263/424/6/55/545/619/20/5/6/37; Stanier LMS 8F 2-8-0: 48033/164/7/99/210/3/331/41/6/60/515/39/45/6/604/10/63. Total: 71

Locomotives allocated to 41E Barrow Hill as per 1st May 1965. Deeley Midland 0F 0-4-0T: 41528/33; Johnson Midland 1F 0-6-0T: 41708/34/63/804/35; Kitson LMS 0F 0-4-0ST: 47001/5; Ivatt LMS 4MT 2-6-0: 43062/80/2/4/9/111/43/53/9/61; WD 2-8-0: 90084/5/9/190/340/68/474/91/509/29/72/3/87/730; Clayton Type 1 diesel electric Bo-Bo: D8604-16. Total: 46.

Locomotives allocated to 41E Barrow Hill as per 5th November 1966: Andrew Barclay 204hp diesel mechanical 0-6-0: D2400/1/2/3/7/9; BR/English Electric 350hp diesel electric 0-6-0: D3252/663/4038/45/72/91/2; BR/Sulzer Type 2 diesel electric Bo-Bo: D7602/3/4/5/6/7/8; English Electric Type 1 diesel electric Bo-Bo: D8060/1/2/3/7/128/9/30/1/2/3. Total: 31.

BARROW HILL SHED BASH 1

TOP: Former Crosti-boilered 9F 2-10-0 No. 92027 shares the loco yard by the ash plant with 8F and WD 2-8-0s on 28th April 1962. On the extreme right can just be seen Engine Shed Sidings signal box which controlled the connections between the depot and the former Springwell branch, and which is still there to this day. *John Beaumont/Robert Anderson Collection*

BELOW: Class 0F 0-4-0ST No. 41518 set against Midland architecture looks elderly but these engines were younger than the 1F 0-6-0Ts, being of a type introduced by the Midland Railway in 1897. No. 41518 was one of only two survivors by the time of this picture on Sunday 21st August 1955. *Neville Stead Collection/Transport Library*

BARROW HILL SHED BASH 11
ABOVE: With the tall chimneys of the Campbell Brickworks as a backdrop, Garratt No. 47973 rests in the yard. The rotary coal bunker is easily visible. These monsters had a phenomenal tractive effort of 45,620lbs. *P.J.Hughes/Colour-Rail*

BELOW: When Sheffield Millhouses shed was closed in January 1962, some of its Class 6 and 7 express locomotives were transferred to Sheffield Darnall. They spent most of their time there in store, being farmed out to various depots in the 41 district including Canklow, Staveley Central and Barrow Hill. One such was Royal Scot No. 46164 *The Artists' Riflemen.* There are no details with this picture but, displaying her 41A shedplate, she looks in good, clean, well-oiled condition though she appears not to be in steam with no lamps and little or no coal in the tender. *Tom Greaves*

BARROW HILL SHED BASH 111

ABOVE: The driver oils round as 8F 2-8-0 No. 48200 is prepared for duty on one of the local trip workings that plied around the area. A selection of wagons occupy the brickworks sidings up on the bank.
Tom Greaves

RIGHT: Up on another bank, 0F 0-4-0T No. 41528 is on duty at the coal stage.
Tom Greaves

BARROW HILL SHED BASH 1V

LEFT: Even a little 0F 0-4-0ST looks big from this angle. The Campbell Brickworks chimneys reach for the sky and No. 47005 looks to be trying to join them while shunting the coal stage. Introduced in 1932, these were not old engines, and 47005 was the first of a batch built as late as 1953 with extended side tanks and increased space for coal *Tom Greaves*

BELOW: An open day on 27th September 1970 saw this beast at Barrow Hill - the opposite end of the scale to 47005 above. The Brush 4,000hp prototype HS4000 *Kestrel* pictured in the BR photograph was undergoing trials from neighbouring Shirebrook depot at the time. After the trials, which raised considerable concern over the effects of its heavy axle load on the track, *Kestrel* was sold to the Soviet Union.

ABOVE: It's a tight fit on the turntable for BREL Doncaster-built 58041 *Ratcliffe Power Station* on Saturday 15th December 1990. Although closure was a couple of months away, locomotives were no longer maintained in the roundhouse - that work having gone to Shirebrook - and they were brought in specially for the photographer.

RIGHT: Some of the last men at Barrow Hill. From left they are: train crew supervisor Donald Meggitt, driver Wilf Nightingale, Worksop freight services manager Roland Walker, senior driver Harry Whatmore and driver Roy Morley.

BELOW: All quiet. The west end of the shed on 15th December 1990.
All Stephen Chapman

ABOVE: At Barrow Hill Junction an 8F 2-8-0, No. 48210, comes off the line from Hall Lane Junction via Summit Sidings with a heavy Up Through Freight, possibly 8M82 the 2.25pm to Washwood Heath, at 2.45pm on Saturday 28th April 1962. The lines in the centre foreground lead into the Staveley Iron & Chemical Works, and via sidings, to the GC Chesterfield Loop. The line turning off to the right just by the tank wagons also leads into the iron and chemical works. *Robert Anderson*

BELOW: During 1964 dirty Sulzer Type 2 No. D5202 passes through Barrow Hill station(Barrow Hill & Staveley Works until 1951) with fully fitted express freight 4M84, the 03.35 Carlisle-St. Pancras due at 15.22. An Ivatt Class 4 2-6-0 waits on the goods only line from Hall Lane Junction via Summit Sidings - this line was shown in both the LMS 1935 and BR 1969 sectional appendices as a Single Goods Line worked by Absolute Block. The 1969 appendix gave a maximum line speed of 25mph. Despite being closed to regular passenger services with effect from 5th July 1954, the platforms are still in good order and the nameboards intact since the station would still be used for excursion trains. *Stephen Chapman archive*

ABOVE: With Barrow Hill Junction signal box on the left, 4F 0-6-0 No. 44066 draws Target 59 out of Barrow Hill station sidings en-route to Dunston & Barlow at 1.15pm on Saturday 6th October 1962. *Robert Anderson*

BELOW: Original Midland 4F No. 43869 at work in Summit Sidings during 1960. An earlier trip numbering system was in use then and she is on Target 136 which saw the specified "Class 4 freight engine" leave Barrow Hill shed at 6.40am and run light to Summit Sidings. She would then make five return trips to Markham Colliery until 11.10 am when she was available to work as required, not returning to the shed until 2am next day. Summit Sidings provided an exchange with the Staveley Iron & Chemical Co.'s works. *Tom Greaves*

ABOVE: Storming southbound through Barrow Hill station at 5.55pm on Saturday 6th October 1962 is 8F 2-8-0 No. 48508 with an Up class 5 freight(vacuum brake operative on at least half the vehicles.) *Robert Anderson*

BELOW: WD 2-8-0 No. 90318 has just passed through Barrow Hill station with its Down loaded mineral train on the "Old Road" at 1.10pm on Saturday 26th May 1962. On the left is the 1745-yard single line from Barrow Hill Junction to Hall Lane Junction avoiding Summit Sidings. This line was once used by Chesterfield-Mansfield passenger trains. *Robert Anderson*

ABOVE: Ivatt Class 4 2-6-0 No. 43090 drifts gently down from the Hall Lane direction towards the "Old Road" at Barrow Hill Junction with a trip working at 5.20pm on Saturday 6th October 1962. *Robert Anderson*

BARROW HILL TRIP DUTIES 1963. Target 59 made several runs to Oxcroft Colliery before making an afternoon run to Dunston & Barlow, or Hollis Lane on Saturdays; **Target 60** worked Barrow Hill-Dunston & Barlow and Whittington; **Target 61**made runs between Barrow Hill, Chesterfield, Hollis Lane and Tapton Junction; **Target 62** served Ireland Colliery several times during its 13 1/2-hour shift; **Target 63** was booked for just one run from Barrow Hill Down Sidings to Seymour Junction at 6.40am; **Target 64** in its 13-hour shift first went to Markham Colliery, then to Glapwell Colliery and back, and then a return trip to the Distillates Plant at Bolsover before visiting Bolsover Coalite Sidings; **Target 66** ran back and forth between Summit Sidings and Markham Colliery; **Target 67**: ran back and forth between Seymour Jn. and Glapwell Colliery; **Target 68** comprised a single run of empties from Barrow Hill Up Sidings to Seymour Jn.; **Target 69** made similar runs as Target 64 but with an afternoon visit to Ramcroft Colliery; **Target 71** ran to Renishaw Park Goods Jn.(for Renishaw Park Colliery)and back in the morning and then as far north as Woodhouse Mill in the afternoon, returning in the evening; **Target 72** worked back and forth between Seymour Jn., Bolsover Coalite and Barrow Hill Up Sidings.
Trips originating from Hasland and depots outside the area included: **Target 18** making return trips between Avenue Sidings and Seymour Jn. or Barrow Hill; **Target 24** from Wincobank Sidings(near Meadow Hall) to Renishaw Park Goods; and **Target 25**, a class 7 from Sheffield Engine Shed Sidings to Seymour Jn.

RIGHT: Staveley iron works dominates the skyline as 8F 2-8-0 No. 48144 storms a coal train away from Hall Lane and towards Barrow Hill at 3.36pm on 6th October 1962. The line to Summit Sidings is on the right. *Robert Anderson*

ABOVE: Among the fields, 4F 0-6-0 No. 44437 heads empty mineral wagons from Barrow Hill Junction towards Hall Lane Junction at 2.50pm on 6th October 1962. This line, which avoided Summit Sidings, was listed in the 1935 LMS Sectional Appendix as a single line worked by Token. The 1969 BR Appendix showed it as a single line worked by Absolute Block. Despite the intense heavy industry of the Chesterfield and Staveley area with iron works, chemical works, coking plants and collieries, the landscape remained surprisingly rural. Through the smoke in the left background is a row of houses called Devonshire Villas. *Robert Anderson*

BELOW: Well, mostly rural. Looking the other way from the above picture reveals a landscape somewhat disfigured by industry with Staveley Works and slag tips on each side of the line. Target 67 headed by 4F No. 44475 is returning to Barrow Hill at 4pm on Saturday 6th October 1962 after spending its shift tripping between Seymour Junction and Glapwell Colliery. The line to Barrow Hill via Summit Sidings comes straight ahead on the right.
Hall Lane Junction and signal box are in the distance, just beyond the double decker bridge. The lower bridge carries Hall Lane over the railway and the more prominent higher bridge the Staveley Works internal railway to sidings in the slag tipping and crushing area on the left, from where a line continues over the "Old Road" at Foxlow Junction to another slag tip. *Robert Anderson*

ABOVE: Three lines met at Hall Lane Junction, the other was a curve from Rotherham-facing Foxlow Junction on the "Old Road." Together, they formed a triangle between the "Old Road" and Hall Lane Junction. In this view from the same spot as the previous two, a 4F 0-6-0 ambles along beneath the slag crushing works with a train of 16-ton mineral wagons from Foxlow Junction towards Hall Lane Junction at 4pm on 6th October 1962. *Robert Anderson*

RIGHT: Ivatt Class 4 2-6-0 No. 43090 makes a big show as it works flat out onto the Summit Sidings line with a heavy load of coal from Seymour Junction at 4.10pm on 6th October 1962. *Robert Anderson*

BR ENGINES AT STAVELEY IRON & CHEMICAL WORKS

ABOVE: 1F 0-6-0Ts Nos. 41875(left) and 41804 come together deep in the Staveley Works complex at 2.20pm on Saturday 6th October 1962. 41875 is still wearing a 41D Canklow shedplate, its previous home. Just above 41875's cab roof and first wagon can be seen the blast furnaces. *Robert Anderson*

BELOW: The driver of 1F tank No. 41835 looks to the grey yonder on what would appear to be a blustery day while dealing with a 27-ton iron ore tippler. No. 41835 had also previously been a Canklow engine - the Staveley Works requirement ensured that these Barrow Hill engines outlived their classmates by a fair margin. *Tom Greaves*

ABOVE: A vast array of newly manufactured tubes and pipes can be seen from the elevated prospect where 0F 0-4-0T No. 41528 is shunting a variety of wagons. A steam crane is at work in the right distance. The blast furnaces at Staveley were closed in the early 1960s following takeover by Stewarts & Lloyds and merger with the Stanton Iron Co. to form Stanton & Staveley. A new chemical plant was established on the site of the furnaces in 1966. *Tom Greaves*

BOTTOM: No. 41804 eases a rake of BR mineral wagons past an interesting selection of rail cranes, at least two steam and one derelict, outside the engine shed on Saturday 8th May 1965. *From a colour slide. Stephen Chapman archive*

ABOVE: Amid the clutter one might expect to find in a works manufacturing tubes and pipes, 0F 0-4-0T No. 41529 sits outside one of the site's two engine sheds alongside one of the works' own industrial shunters. By the mid-1970s the works, by then called Staveley Foundry was part of Stanton & Staveley, a subsidiary of the British Steel Corporation. It had four Sentinel diesel hydraulic shunters built around 1960 of its own but was still hiring from BR. It became part of Stanton plc in 1985 upon privatisation of British Steel. The last remains of the works closed in 2012, around 26 years after rail traffic had ended. *Neville Stead collection/Transport Library*

BOTTOM: No. 41804 moves internal wagon No. 1423 over one of the access roads to Staveley New Works at 12.10pm on Saturday 28th May 1962. The direction sign reads Foundry B straight ahead and Devonshire Works to the right. There are frequent Devonshire references around the area, the Dukes of Devonshire at nearby Chatsworth House being major landowners with considerable interests in local industry. On the right are an engine shed, a crane and internal wagon F147. *Robert Anderson*

ABOVE: When one sees the scale of huge industrial plants such as this it is not readily appreciated that when it comes to it, they produce the everyday items we are all familiar with. In this view of 41835 propelling loaded BR wagons past the cooling towers at 4.30pm on 8th October 1962, it would appear that weedkiller, or an ingredient in its composition, was a product of the chemical works if the Chipman's tank wagon on the extreme right is anything to go by. *Robert Anderson*

BELOW: The now preserved 1F 0-6-0T No. 41708 keeps one of the works' own 0-4-0 saddletanks company in 1961 outside the engine shed shown in the picture opposite. Good to see that both were smartly turned out. *From a Colour-Rail colour slide*

ABOVE: East of Hall Lane Junction, the line to Seymour Junction was double track. On 6th September 1959 Midland 4F No. 43869 and its train of empty mineral wagons going in the Seymour Junction direction are just passing over the Chesterfield Canal bridge and are about to pass under the Great Central main line, and then pass the closed Staveley Town station. The houses of Franklyn Drive are in the immediate right background and in front of them passed the single line to a north-facing junction on the GC main line. The houses visible beyond the wagons are Hartington Cottages which had been demolished by the 1970s. *Peter Hay/Transport Library*

BELOW: Seymour Junction was where the line to Elmton & Creswell via Clowne parted company from the line to Bolsover and Glapwell Colliery. It was an important centre for marshalling traffic from the various local collieries and remained so until the demise of coal traffic during the course of the 1990s. Also here at one time were Seymour Colliery and, later, a coal stocking ground. On Saturday 16th October 1965, it was visited by 1X20 the Midland Requiem railtour from Nuneaton run by the Railway Correspondence & Travel Society and hauled by 4F 0-6-0 No. 43953, one of the last three surviving Midland Railway 4Fs by that time. BR required that diesel assistance be provided in the shape of Clayton Type 1(Class 17) No. D8613 from Seymour Junction to Glapwell Colliery, but contrary to normal practice, the steam engine was leading. For the return run the inspector(is that him in the trilby?) was persuaded to allow 43953 to work back without the diesel pilot. *From a colour slide by K.C.H. Fairey/Colour-Rail*

RIGHT: In the early 1960s, LMS 4F No. 44265 is busy at Seymour Junction with Target 67 which serviced Glapwell Colliery. The driver and his young fireman are taking a keen interest in the activity on the right. It looks like permanent way work but in fact a derailment is being dealt with. *Tom Greaves*

BELOW: Bolsover Coalite and Chemical Works in the 1980s. Seen from Buttermilk Lane overbridge, a pair of Class 20s are heading for Seymour Junction with a train of loaded air braked hopper wagons while older 21/24-ton vacuum braked hoppers are in the sidings on the right. *S. Chapman archive*

ABOVE: Immediately north of Buttermilk Lane, the Midland Requiem railtour of 16th October 1965 threads its way through the less than scenic, but no doubt fascinating to some, Bolsover Coalite & Chemical landscape with 43953 leading D8613. No. 43953 must have been adjudged to be in the best condition of the three surviving Midland 4Fs as it had been specially brought from Workington for the job. Even so, it was withdrawn just three weeks later along with the other two, 43906 and 43968. *Mike Mitchell/Transport Treasury*

BELOW: A more sylvan setting at Bolsover Coalite works where Thomas Hill 0-6-0 diesel 238v of 1971 shunts internal hopper wagons loaded with coke on Bank Holiday Monday 31st May 1982. The level crossing is for an internal road. *Adrian Booth*

ABOVE: At Bolsover Castle, signalman Boden exchanges tokens with the Midland Requiem railtour crew on D8613, allowing it to proceed to Glapwell Colliery at 15.36 on Saturday 16th October 1965. *Robert Anderson*

BELOW: Bolsover Castle station with 43953 and The Midland Requiem on its return run, minus the Clayton diesel, at 15.55 on 16th October 1965. Bolsover was listed in the 1956 Handbook of Stations as being able to handle parcels, miscellaneous traffic and livestock only. It had closed to passengers on 28th July 1930 and closed completely on 1st November 1962. *Robert Anderson*

ABOVE: Another railtour to Glapwell Colliery and gricerly invasion as seen on Sunday 24th July 1960 with 4F 0-6-0 No. 44590 piloting an Ivatt Class 4 2-6-0. The view is of the colliery sidings immediately south of the former junction with the rest of the line going on to Pleasley which closed in the 1930s. *From a Colour-Rail colour slide*

LEFT: An old late 19th or early 20th century postcard view of Glapwell station, similar in style to Bolsover. Glapwell was listed in the 1938 Handbook of Stations as being equipped to handle parcels and miscellaneous traffic only. It closed to passengers when the Mansfield service was withdrawn on 28th July 1930 and completely on 23rd September 1946. *Railway Station Photographs*

The BR 1969 Sectional Appendix showed the **Seymour Junction-Glapwell Colliery branch**(often referred to as the Doe Lea branch) as a single line worked by Electric Token between Markham Colliery Sidings and Glapwell Colliery. Between Seymour Jn. and Markham Colliery it consisted of a bi-directional single goods line worked by Absolute Block plus a bi-directional Up line worked by Absolute Block. The maximum line speed was 30mph. There were signal boxes at Markham Colliery Sidings (1351yds from Seymour Jn.,) Bolsover Castle(1 mile 1065yds from Markham Colliery,) and Glapwell Colliery Sidings(1mile 1665yds from Bolsover.) **The Ireland Colliery branch** was worked under One Engine in Steam regulations with a 15mph maximum speed. The branch from **Markham Colliery Sidings to Markham Colliery No.2 Pit** was worked as a single line under Permissive Block regulations with Electric Token. There was a token station at the New Loaded Wagon Weigh Office(438yds from Markham Colliery Sidings signal box.) The maximum permissible speed was 15mph. The 1935 LMS Sectional Appendix also showed a location at Ramcroft Colliery Junction(which was not a block post) and the colliery branch worked by Train Staff.

Palterton & Sutton station between Glapwell and Bolsover was 1545yds from Ramcroft Colliery Junction. It also closed to passengers on 28th July 1930. The 1938 Handbook of Stations listed it as being able to handle general goods, livestock, furniture vans, carriages, motor cars and machines on wheels. Goods facilities were withdrawn in December 1939.

Bolsover private sidings 1956: NCB Bolsover Colliery & Brickworks; British Diesel Oil & Petrol Co. Ltd, Covert Siding; Refinery Sidings; Coalite & Chemical Products Ltd; Derbyshire Coalite Co. Ltd; Glapwell Colliery; Ramcroft Colliery; New Byron Brick Co.'s Siding.

From the 1890s to the 1930s an industrial tramway ran from Bolsover Colliery and Brickworks to the model village of New Bolsover(completed 1896) where it extended along the streets of houses being built around a green quadrangle. It delivered bricks for construction. After completion it supplied coal to the workers who lived there and took away the night soil from the earth privvies.

The 1969 Eastern Region Sectional Appendix shows the **Seymour Junction to Elmton & Creswell** line as a single passenger line signalled by Electric Token. The one intermediate signal box was Oxcroft Colliery Sidings No.3 which was 3 miles one yard from Seymour Jn. The next box was Elmton & Creswell on the Worksop-Mansfield line(2 miles 1164yds from Oxcroft.) The maximum line speed by then was just 25mph. In steam days a banking engine was often needed on the rear of heavier trains ascending the gradient from Elmton & Creswell to Clowne.

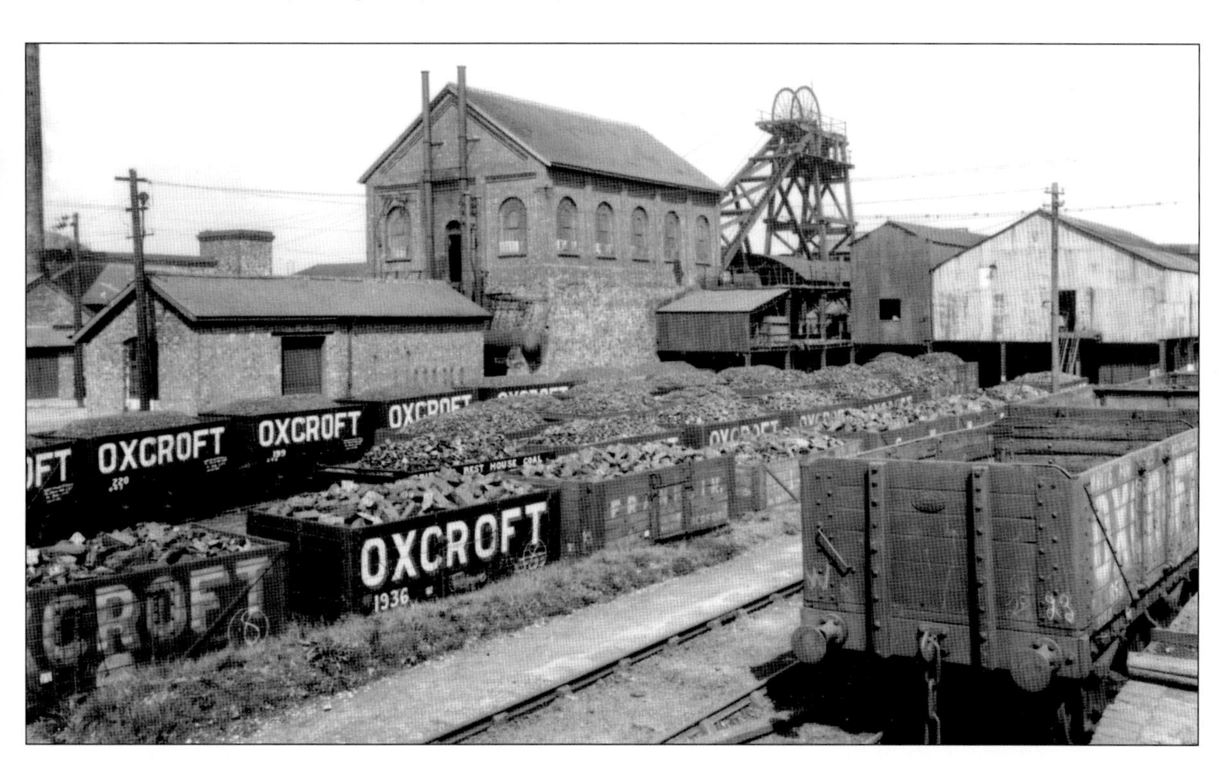

ABOVE: An old undated postcard view of the colliery yard at Oxcroft Colliery. *Ray Woodmore colln.* **The colliery sidings were at the end of a short branch from the Seymour Jn.-Clowne line. From the sidings an internal line crossed the Clowne-Bolsover road into the colliery yard. The 1969 BR Sectional Appendix showed the branch as worked by One Engine Steam regulations, maximum speed, 15mph.**

RIGHT: Following closure of Oxcroft Colliery and establishment of a surface extraction operation, all railway was cut back to a loading bunker on the site of the colliery sidings north of the road. This operation, latterly by Burrows Bros., was soon to cease when this shot of Vulcan Foundry/English Electric 0-6-0 diesel hydraulic 3994 of 1970 and a single MGR hopper was captured on Wednesday 9th November 2005. *Stephen Chapman*

ABOVE: This late Victorian postcard looking west at Clowne(sometimes referred to in official railway publications as Clown) shows Southgate Colliery(closed c1929) on the right and the LD&EC Clowne South station on the far left. Next to it in the centre left, the light patch denotes the Midland Clowne & Barlborough station and goods yard. This goods yard was listed in the 1938 Handbook of Stations as having a permanent 1 1/2-ton crane and equipped to handle all classes of goods except furniture vans, carriages, motor cars and machines on wheels - one can surmise it had no vehicle dock. It closed on 29th October 1951.The 1935 LMS Sectional Appendix stated that the engine must be at the Elmton & Creswell end of "all vehicles taken to or from 'Clown' station sidings, the LNE Co.'s sidings and the Elmton... end of Southgate Colliery sidings." It also stated that all wagons passing between the LNER sidings and Southgate Colliery must be worked by LMS engines.The passenger station closed when the line's remaining regular service was withdrawn on 5th July 1954 but remained available for excursion trains. Curiously, wagons are parked on the main running line. Was shunting in progress or were they placed there for the benefit of Mr. Rogers, the photographer? *Railway Station Photographs*

BELOW: Back on the "Old Road," just over two miles north of Barrow Hill, English Electric Type 1s Nos. 20087 and 20151 head a northbound vacuum braked freight past Renishaw Park on Wednesday 2nd June 1982. Renishaw Park Goods Junction is just beyond the far end of the train. On the right, an industrial loco sits in freshly laid exchange sidings at Renishaw Park Colliery. *Adrian Booth*

RIGHT: Shunting MGR hoppers in the exchange sidings at Renishaw Park Colliery with NCB Hudswell, Clarke diesel 1387 of 1967 on 2nd June 1982. The girder bridge once carried the Great Central line into the colliery which had been removed by the early 1960s. *Adrian Booth*

BELOW: A Victorian postcard view of Eckington & Renishaw station looking north. Renamed from just Eckington in 1880, the station was well equipped to handle all classes of passenger and goods traffic, the yard having a 7-ton permanent crane. Passenger and goods facilities were both withdrawn with effect from 1st October 1951. *Railway Station Photographs*

ABOVE: An Up class 4 fully fitted express goods headed by New England 9F 2-10-0 No. 92182 about to cross the River Rother just south of Killamarsh at 3.13pm on 24th November 1962. *Robert Anderson*

TAPTON JUNCTION TO CHINLEY

BELOW: First station on the new main line to Sheffield after leaving Tapton Junction was Sheepbridge & Whittington Moor, just Sheepbridge from 1951, seen here looking towards Sheffield. It was listed in the 1956 Handbook of Stations as equipped to deal only with passengers, parcels, miscellaneous traffic, general goods and livestock. It had no goods yard and was closed completely with effect from 2nd January 1967 when local services were withdrawn. *Railway Station Photographs*

ABOVE: After Sheepbridge station came the abandoned line going east to the long closed Broomhouse Colliery followed by the lesser of the two tunnels between Tapton and Dore. When 92-yard Broomhouse Tunnel needed major repairs, BR decided the best option was to open it out into a cutting. By Tuesday 19th August 1969 when BR photographer Robert Anderson caught a Sulzer "Peak" Type 4 heading the 09.50 St. Pancras-Leeds at around 12.25 - if on time, the massive 80,000 cubic-yard overburden had been removed ready for demolition.

BELOW: The work required a three-week possession during which trains were diverted via the "Old Road" and on Friday 29th August the tunnel structure was removed using dynamite. That dramatic moment is captured by Robert Anderson in this BR photograph. The picture clearly illustrates the amount of overburden which had to be removed prior to demolition. The line reopened on 7th September.

ABOVE: Unstone Viaduct carries the line over the valley of the River Drone and is pictured here being crossed by a BR/Sulzer "Peak" Type 4 with brake tenders fore and aft on a southbound train of mineral wagons. It has just passed the site of Unstone station and is about to pass Unstone Colliery Sidings signal box, the sidings beginning to the right of the box. *Tom Greaves*

BELOW: About to pass Dronfield station - the goods yard is on the left and the signal box in the right distance - is 22A Barrow Road Jubilee 4-6-0 No. 45660 *Rooke* with an express from Bristol on Wednesday 13th August 1952. *E.R. Morten Collection.* **Dronfield goods yard was listed in the 1956 Handbook of Stations as having a one ton permanent crane and equipped to handle general goods and livestock only. There were private sidings for Henry Boot & Sons Ltd., The English Steel Corporation, and E&W Lucas. There was also Callywhite public siding on the surviving rump, at the Dronfield end, of the Unstone Colliery line. Goods facilities closed on 1st May 1967 and Callywhite Siding on 9th June 1969.**

In 1965 an engine was booked to run from Tinsley diesel depot to Unstone Colliery Sidings where it arrived at 05.18 to collect empty coaches which it then took to Chesterfield to form the summer Saturday 07.15 Chesterfield-St. Pancras. A similar diagram was still running in 1969, an engine arriving from Sheffield Midland at 07.04 and taking empty coaches to Chesterfield to form the summer Saturday 09.15 to Skegness.

The Unstone Colliery line c1900. *Not to scale.* In Lounds Wood, on the opposite side of the Sheffield main line, a tramway ran from a small drift mine.

Day Hole drift mine
Tramway
Summerlee Colliery (closed)
Unstone Colliery here by 1918
Colonial Sanitary Works
Cliffe Iron & Brass foundry
Callywhite Lane
Unstone Main Colliery(closed)
Unstone Colliery (closed)
Ramshaw Wood
Dronfield Engineering Works(disused)
Dronfield
Unstone Sidings
Unstone Station
Signal Box
To Sheffield
©Stephen Chapman 2019
Viaduct
Unstone Jn.
From Tapton Jn

Unstone station *was listed in the 1938 Handbook of Stations as being equipped to handle passengers and general goods only. The goods yard of four sidings had no permanent crane. The station closed to passengers on 29th October 1951 and to goods on 1st September 1961. The platform housed a lever frame which controlled the goods yard sidings, movements being protected by a home signal also worked from the frame. The colliery sidings were controlled from Unstone Colliery Sidings signal box.*

RIGHT: Just north of Dronfield at Holmley Common, alongside Dronfield Forge, a derailed wagon lying "askew" the track is being jacked back into position as Ivatt 2-6-0 No. 43080 waits for the order to move it out of the way and into the sidings. The space beyond the wagon was once occupied by a loading dock for small local collieries. Later, to the left of the line, was the larger but short-lived Dronfield Silkstone Colliery, closed by 1898.
Tom Greaves

BELOW: Dronfield station looks well patronised as a Derby Works DMU set pulls in with a service from Sheffield. The station closed to passengers on 2nd January 1967 and no surprise that it reopened 13 years later.
Railway Station Photographs

ABOVE: In the 1960s when B1 4-6-0s allocated to Canklow shed were to be found on Hope Valley stopping services. No. 61315 has just left Dore & Totley and is approaching Totley Tunnel East with the refuge siding on the right. *Tom Greaves*

LEFT: In this picture, an express hauled by "Black Five" 4-6-0 No. 45133 is bursting out of 3 mile 950yd Totley Tunnel and is about to pass through Grindleford station. The pediment on the tunnel declares 1893, the year the Dore & Chinley line opened. *Tom Greaves*

The Dore & Chinley line was listed in the 1935 LMS Sectional Appendix as worked by Absolute Block. The Up direction was from Chinley. Signal boxes(with distance from previous box) were at: Chinley East Jn.(533yds from Chinley North Jn.;) Cowburn Tunnel West(1628yds.;) Cowburn Tunnel East(2m 934yds;) Edale(1699yds;) Norman's Bank(2m 1336yds.;) Earle's Sidings(1m 482yds.;) Hope(1m 166yds.;) Bamford Water Board Sidings(1m 135yds.;) Bamford(1159yds.;) Hathersage(1m 1424yds.;) Grindleford(1m 1245yds.;) Totley Tunnel East(4m 229yds;) Dore & Totley West Jn.(998yds.;) Dore & Totley South Jn.(419yds.)
Refuge(lie-by) sidings were at: Cowburn Tunnel West (Up) 40 wagons; Cowburn Tunnel East(Down) 34 wagons,) Edale(37 wagons Up, 40 wagons Down,) Hope(38 wagons Up, 32 wagons Down,) Bamford(43 wagons Up, 37 wagons Down,) Hathersage(43 wagons Up, 33 wagons Down,) Grindleford(Up)40 wagons, Totley Tunnel East(Down) 35 wagons.

ABOVE: Grindleford station looking west in June 1960 with Fairburn 2-6-4T No. 42109 on a local service to Sheffield. The goods yard and warehouse are on the left. Could the boys on the platform be going spotting at Sheffield Midland? *Neville Stead Collection/Transport Library*

LEFT: The goods warehouse has gone but Grindleford still retains much of its traditional character in this Saturday 7th May 1988 view of Brush Type 2 No. 31441 passing through on the 13.45 Sheffield-Liverpool. The sidings on the left were once linked to an inclined tramway which came down just alongside the top left hand corner of 31441's cab. It brought stone down from a quarry which was then taken to sidings between Bamford and Hope where it was transferred to a light railway which took the stone up to the construction sites of the Derwent and Ladybower reservoirs. *From a colour slide by Stephen Chapman*

On weekdays in summer 1961 from 6.30am to 9.47pm, Grindleford station saw 10 departures for Chinley.The 8.16am and 5.59pm were advertised as having through carriages to Manchester Central via Stockport Tiviot Dale. There were nine departures towards Sheffield from 7.45am to 9.4pm. The 4.59pm was advertised as having through carriages from Stockport Tiviot Dale, and likewise the 5.9 and the 5.42pm from Manchester Central via Stockport Tiviot Dale. The 9.30pm Manchester Central-Sheffield passed through non-stop. There were extra trains on Saturdays and nine trains each way on Sundays. **Grindleford goods yard** was listed in 1956 as having a 4-ton crane and equipped for general goods traffic only. It stayed in business for domestic coal until the 1980s but the station lost its staff in 1969.

LEFT: The style of Hathersage station was similar to the others on the line. Seen here is 4F 0-6-0 No. 44229, slogging through the station with an Avenue Sidings-Gowhole coal train. *Tom Greaves*

Hathersage goods yard was at the east end of the station and included a 10-ton crane, loading dock and vehicle dock. It was listed in 1956 as equipped to handle all classes of goods. Goods facilities were withdrawn with effect from 30th January 1965. The station became unstaffed in September 1969.

BELOW: A stopping service from Sheffield headed by 4F No. 44606 calls at Bamford in Whit. Monday 6th June 1960. The signal box and goods yard can be seen in the background. *Neville Stead collection/ Transport Library*

Bamford had well appointed goods facilities and was listed in 1956 as possessing a 5-ton permanent crane and being able to handle all classes of goods.Goods facilities here were withdrawn from 31st January 1966. The station was also destaffed in September 1969.

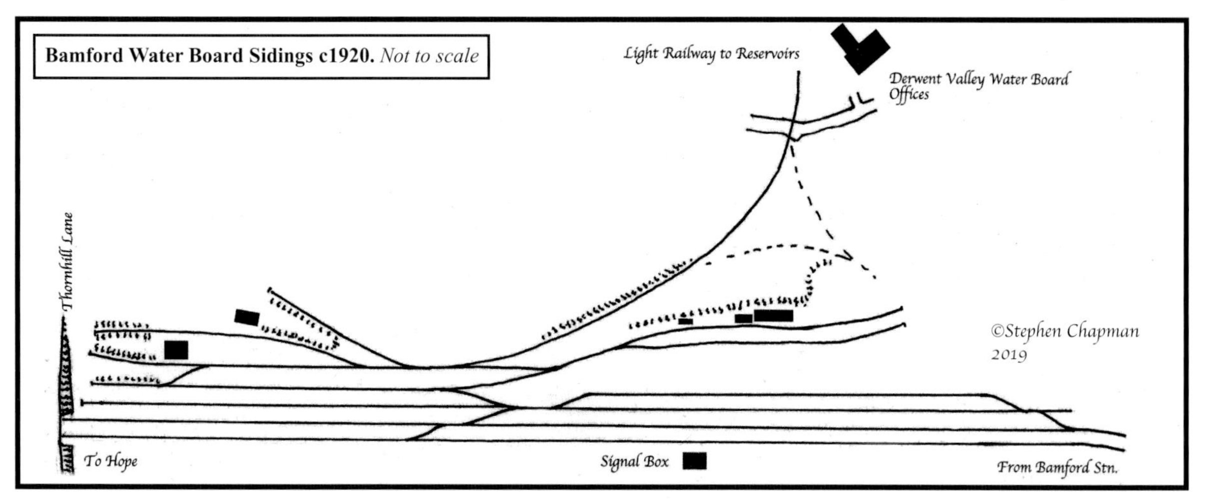

LEFT: Evidently, the temporary standard gauge light railway which climbed up from Water Board Sidings to the construction sites of Howden and Derwent reservoirs in the early 1900s ran a passenger service for workers and their families. The note with this old postcard view states Birchinlea which was effectively the end of the line but it appears to be the temporary settlement at Derwent Farm. The 0-4-0ST is unidentified but clearly has Peckett styling. *Railway Station Photographs*

RIGHT: Hope station looking east with mailbags on the Sheffield platform and a brake van in the siding at the platform end. As with the others, Hope became unstaffed in 1969 and subsequently its charming buildings were demolished but the footbridge survives.
Goods facilities, which were beyond the footbridge, could handle all classes of traffic but there was no permanent crane. They were withdrawn on 20th April 1964.
Railway Station Photographs

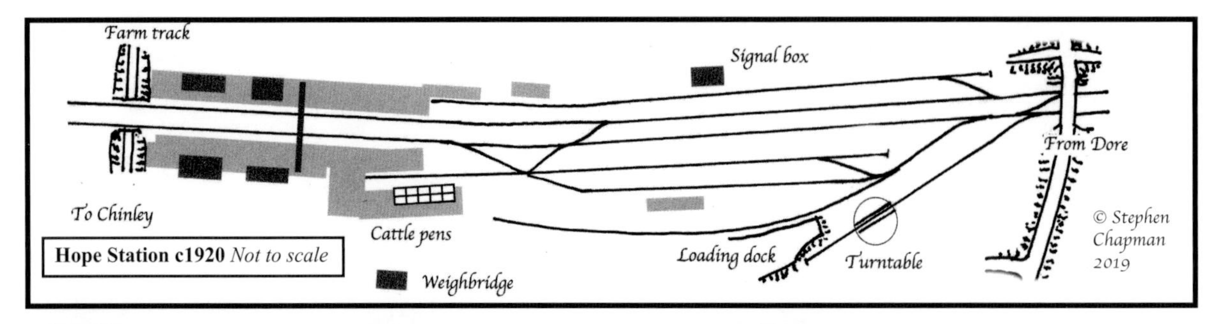

LEFT: From Earle's Sidings, west of Hope station, runs a 11/4-mile private industrial branch line to what was originally Earle's cement factory, but which has since its opening in 1929 seen several changes of ownership. In 1990 the then owners Blue Circle ordered the unique B-B diesel hydraulic locomotive *Blue John* from Hunslet-Barclay, Kilmarnock, builders No. 773. It is seen here on 11th August 1997 crossing the footpath which leads from Hope village to Castleton while hauling empty cement tanks from the main line at Earle's Sidings. Being a "one-off" spares became hard to come by and *Blue John* was out of use at the time of writing, replaced by ex-BR class 20s. *From a colour slide by Stephen Chapman*

ABOVE: Class 8F 2-8-0 No. 48191 blasts up the 1 in 100 through Edale station with a heavy westbound train of loaded Presflo cement wagons from Earle's Sidings. Edale was able to handle all classes of goods but had no permanent crane. Goods facilities, west of the station, were withdrawn from 7th October 1963 but an odd siding survived into the 21st century, for years occupied by an old parcels van but since disconnected from the main lines. *Railway Station Photographs*

RIGHT: Chinley North Junction and its original Midland Railway signal box before its replacement with the standard London Midland Region flat-roof variety. The "Peak" is coming round off the Matlock line while the Hope Valley line curves away left. The telegraph poles are another once familiar lineside feature which has mostly disappeared. *The late Jack Wild/Stephen Chapman Archive*

CENTRE: Among facilities for terminating and starting passenger trains at Chinley were its turntable and carriage siding. "Spinner" 4-2-2 No. 627, still in Midland Railway livery, is seen on the turntable in 1924. *Neville Stead collection/ Transport Library*

BELOW: BR Standard Class 5 4-6-0 No. 73144 - one of those fitted with Caprotti valve gear - rolls into Chinley with a westbound class 8 unfitted goods on Sunday 12th March 1961. Since 73144 is a Rowsley engine the train has obviously come off the Matlock line.
Stephen Chapman archive

ABOVE: Nottingham-allocated LMS-built 4P Compound 4-4-0 No. 41185 leaves Chinley's six-platform station and heads back to the East Midlands with a stopping service on Tuesday 7th June 1960 while 4F 0-6-0 No. 44162 sits on the turntable road. Another eastbound train, presumably a Sheffield service, sits in the station. Beyond 41185 is Chinley Station South signal box.
Neville Stead collection/Transport Library

BELOW: The scene at Chinley on Saturday 20th April 1968. Well-groomed "Black Five" 4-6-0s Nos. 45110 and 44949 call with the North West Railtour run by the Severn Valley Railway Society and Manchester Rail Travel Society. The "Black Fives" worked the Stockport-Buxton-Peak Forest-Guide Bridge-Stalybridge portion of this epic which started and terminated at Birmingham New Street.
From a Stephen Chapman archive colour slide

RIGHT: Trafford Park's 4P Compound 4-4-0 No. 40910 awaits departure from Chinley with a stopping service to Manchester in the 1950s. The goods shed and 5-ton yard crane are on the right. Despite these facilities, Chinley was listed in 1956 as only being able to handle general goods. The 1938 Handbook of Stations listed it as also being able to handle livestock and horse boxes and prize cattle vans, a service which had been withdrawn in the intervening years. All goods facilities were with withdrawn with effect from 7th October 1963. *Tom Greaves*

BELOW: With the full layout of Chinley stretched out behind it, 8F 2-8-0 No. 48494 from Toton depot heads a mineral trip towards Gowhole yard at 4.53pm on Saturday 4th May 1963. The goods shed is being used as a carriage siding while a B1 4-6-0 that will probably work the coaches back to Sheffield stands beyond it. Chinley Station North signal box is on the right. *Robert Anderson*

In 1965 *the 06.06 Sheffield-Chinley and 07.40 return were worked by a Canklow B1 until that shed closed, after which they were diesel-hauled, usually by Sulzer Type 2s. The 07.00 Chinley-Sheffield and 09.39 return were worked by Buxton Class 2 2-6-0s. The 13.45 and 16.10 Manchester-Sheffield and 17.30 and 21.22 return were booked for "Black Fives."*

ABOVE: The desolate scene at Chinley on Friday 16th September 1983 after all but the two main running lines had been removed along with the station buildings. BR/Sulzer Type 2 No. 25286 passes through the rubble-strewn platforms with limestone in the LMS/ICI bogie hoppers built in the 1930s for Buxton-Northwich traffic. *From colour slide by Stephen Chapman*

LEFT: The fells of near 1700ft that form a barrier between Chinley and Edale raise a formidable backdrop to Brush Type 2 No. 31422. It has just returned into the sunlight after bringing the 10.45 Liverpool - Yarmouth through the 2 mile 182-yard Cowburn Tunnel on Saturday 7th May 1988. *From colour slide by Stephen Chapman*

THE GREAT CENTRAL LINES

ABOVE: Sheffield Darnall's B1 4-6-0 No. 61044 passes Killamarsh Junction with an Up stopping service. Coming in from the right is the Waleswood curve from Waleswood Junction on the Sheffield-Retford line. The signal that is at danger is for the south-facing junction leading to the LD&EC line to Shirebrook North via Clowne South. *P.J. Hughes/Colour-Rail*

BELOW: A diesel-hauled express on the GC main line in 1961. A southbound train displaying class 1 discs, passes through Killamarsh Central hauled by 1000hp English Electric Type 1(Class 20) No. D8051. In the right background is the goods depot which in 1956 was listed as having a 5 ton permanent crane and able to handle all kind of goods. The passenger station closed with effect from 4th March 1963 and goods facilities from 12th June 1965. On the bridge beyond the goods depot is the line connecting the GC main line to the LD&EC Shirebrook line where it passes over a branch from the LD&EC to Glover's Valley Flour Mills. Killamarsh Station signal box is in the left distance. *From a colour-Rail slide by C. Woodhead.*

PILSLEY-BEIGHTON

BRITISH RAILWAYS EASTERN REGION SECTIONAL APPENDIX 1960

SIGNALLING: Absolute block on Up and Down Main Lines.

MAXIMUM SPEED: On Main Lines: 70mph

Additional lines: Up Goods Loop at Holmewood Colliery, Heath, with room for 88 wagons, engine & brake van. Up and Down Passenger lines Staveley South-North. Down Goods Loop at Staveley with room for 84 wagons, engine & brake van. Up Refuge Siding at Staveley with room for 80 wagons, engine & brake van.

SIGNAL BOXES(with distance from previous box): Holmewood Colliery(1 mile 1608yds from Pilsley;) Heath Station (1080yds;) Heath Junction(505yds;) Duckmanton South Jn.(2miles 991yds;) Duckmanton North Jn.(1119yds;) Staveley South Jn.(2miles 258yds;) Staveley North Jn.(640yds;) Renishaw Central(1mile 1366yds;)Killamarsh Station(1mile 1643yds;) Killamarsh junction(1060yds;) Holbrook Colliery Sidings(1749yds;) Beighton Station Jn.(570yds.)

The 1969 Eastern Region Sectional Appendix showed the surviving 9-mile 288yd line from Beighton Junction to Arkwright Colliery after the 1966 closure as being single line worked in accordance with One Engine in Steam regulations with a maximum speed of 30mph to Duckmanton North ground frame. From there to the colliery it was 15mph.

LEFT: Renishaw Central station (Eckington & Renishaw until September 1950) looking north in the early 1960s. It also closed on 4th March 1963. *Railway Station Photographs*

BELOW: One of J.G. Robinson's sturdy Great Central 2-8-0s, Class 04/1 No. 63692, plods through Renishaw Central on Saturday 2nd March 1963 with an Up class 8 coal train. *Chris Gammell/Photos from the Fifties*

ABOVE: In the bottom right corner, the Midland branch from the "Old Road" to Renishaw Ironworks passes beneath the Great Central main line and Renishaw Central station where another O4 2-8-0, this one an unidentified reboilered version, makes its way northbound with a coal train on Saturday 2nd March 1963. The ice of that severe winter maintains its grip.
Chris Gammell/Photos from the Fifties

BELOW: In this view, the GC branch to Renishaw Ironworks goes off to the right behind Renishaw Central station where another Robinson 2-8-0 version, No. 63773 rebuilt as Class 01, heads light en-route for its home depot at Staveley. It has just passed a northbound coke train headed by Brush Type 2 diesel(Class 31) No. D5836. On the left of this picture is the station goods yard which was listed in 1956 as equipped with a 10-ton crane and able to handle all classes of goods except livestock. It closed on 12th June 1965. *Tom Greaves*

ABOVE: This interesting view at Staveley North Junction on Friday 6th September 1957 shows J11 0-6-0 No. 64433 of 38B Annesley shed with a northbound trip of empty wagons. The line curving away on the right is to Hartington Colliery and the connection with the Midland Barrow Hill-Seymour Junction line which passes underneath the GC main line, the intersection bridge parapets just visible between the brake van and the signal box. The line on the left is a shunting neck for Staveley Traffic Yard. St. John The Baptist's church points the way to Heaven on the hilltop. *Neville Stead collection/Transport Library*

BELOW: Under the LNER and BR in the 1950s, the Great Central came under Great Northern lines management which could lead to an interesting variety of motive power. Here, ex-GN J6 0-6-0 No. 64269 of 38A Colwick shed, passes Staveley North Junction box with a 1950s Sheffield Victoria-Nottingham Victoria local. *Neville Stead collection./Transport Library*

ABOVE: The four-platform Staveley Central looking north in the 1960s. Staveley Traffic Yard is on the far right and the near moribund station goods depot on the left where the 11/2-ton crane has already been dismantled. In 1956 the depot was listed as being equipped to handle all classes of goods. It closed on 12th June 1965, the passenger station having closed on 4th March 1963.
Railway Station Photographs

BELOW: Staveley's own J11 No. 64384 hauls a Down freight through Central station at 11.26am on a dank Saturday 8th October 1960.
Robert Anderson

ABOVE: In this dramatic scene on Saturday 2nd March 1963, two class 8 Through Freights head south from Staveley Central neck and neck under Lowgates Road bridge. On the left Staveley's 04/8 Thompson rebuild 2-8-0 No. 63705 has just come through the station on the Up Slow line while on the right original Robinson GC 04/1 No. 63692 of Retford has the lead while pulling out of the Traffic Yard.

BELOW: Looking south from the above view as 63692 comes up against adverse signals. Through the haze, the motive power depot is on the left while on the right is Staveley South Junction signal box where the Chesterfield Loop diverges right.
Both Chris Gammell/Photos from the Fifties.

Staveley Central was the key operating centre for the GC main line and branches in the Chesterfield area with its motive power depot at the heart of things in much the same way as Barrow Hill on its Midland counterpart. Upon nationalisation, Staveley was coded 38D in the British Railways Eastern Region's Colwick motive power district. Following the 1958 reorganisation, it became 41H in the Sheffield Division. Staveley shed was established by the Manchester, Sheffield & Lincolnshire Railway when its new lines arrived in the area during the early 1890s but the buildings seen here, with northlight roof and shedmaster's office with bay window - along with the huge brick built coaling stage with water tank on top - are standard Great Central and similar could be seen along the route all the way to Neasden. Staveley was primarily a freight shed but had a handful of mixed traffic engines for local passenger duty. It closed when all through freight operations on the GC main line ceased in June 1965. It is still hard to take in that this once busy railway complex has been completely wiped from the face of the earth - now occupied by an industrial estate and new road. South of here, however, it is still possible to travel along the main line - by bike as it has been converted into a cycle track.
ABOVE: A general view of the engine shed on Sunday 3rd May 1964 showing five remaining covered roads after reduction from 12 roads during the early 1950s when the shed was rebuilt. The engines on view are almost entirely 2-8-0s apart from the Brush Type 4 diesel(Class 47) stabled in the roofless area on the right. *From a Colour-Rail colour slide*

STAVELEY TRIP DUTIES 1963

No.21 worked between Staveley, Renishaw and Killamarsh and was booked to be worked by the Renishaw pilot.
No.22 went to Arkwright Colliery and was shown to make tips as required between between Arkwright Colliery and Staveley Central.
No.23 worked between Staveley Central and Staveley Works and Sheepbridge Sidings.
No.24 left Staveley light engine for Chesterfield Central at 9.13am and acted as pilot there until 4.30pm when it returned to Staveley.
No.26 made several trips to Kirkby Bentinck and back again between 6.25am and 4.14pm;
No.27 was the Heath pilot, leaving Staveley with empties at 9.15am and setting off back to Staveley at 3.30pm.
No.28 only ran when required, making a round trip to Pilsley.

On Sundays during the time the Staveley Central South Junction box is closed, engines requiring to travel to or from the Loco Sheds must travel at Caution via the Through line to or from Staveley Central North Junction. All Yard signals will be at Danger, and drivers are authorised to pass these on making sure the line is clear. Drivers must arrange for the fireman to proceed on foot in front of engines in both directions to ensure safety. *BR Eastern Region Sectional Appendix 1960*

LOCOMOTIVES ALLOCATED TO STAVELEY 38D
As per 11th June 1955. 04 2-8-0: 63587/648/75/94/702/5/20/35/49/62/72/87/801/4/27/47/84/99; J11 0-6-0: 64313/7/36/45/84/6/96/433/44; C13 4-4-2T: 67419; J69 0-6-0T: 68512; J67 0-6-0T: 68589; N5 0-6-2T: 69263/69/79/301/51/63; WD 2-8-0: 90115/394/418/60. Total: 40.

LOCOMOTIVES ALLOCATED TO STAVELEY 41H
Summer 1964. 01 2-8-0:63571/89/90/630/46/50/63/725/68/73/86/63/8/79; 04 2-8-0: 63612/701/6/913. Total:18.

Engines Passing Through Traffic Yard. Before engines are allowed to be run over the Through road from North end to South end, the North end staff must advise the South end staff by telephone and obtain permission for this to be done. Similarly, when engines are required to go from South end to North end, the South end staff must advise the North end staff and obtain permission for this to be done.
Drivers must, after receiving instructions to travel from North end to South end of Staveley Central Traffic Yard, stop opposite the Inspector's office at the South end and then work to hand signals. Also, when travelling from South end to North end must stop clear of the fouling point North end of No.11 Siding, and then work to hand signals of North end staff. *BR Eastern Region Sectional Appendix 1960.*

ABOVE: In the later years of steam, Staveley Central was used as a repository for stored and withdrawn locomotives from other sheds in the Sheffield Division. In this view on Easter Monday 30th March 1959 are the grim lines of unwanted engines in a demolished area of the shed, some with their chimneys covered over, a hopeful sign of possible further use when required. They include five "Large Director" D11 4-4-0s from Sheffield Darnall, stored awaiting the recall to duty in the summer.
Neville Stead collection/Transport Library

LEFT: J11 0-6-0 No. 64444 stands by the turntable while being re-stocked with fuel from the massive coaling stage at 11.10am on Saturday 8th October 1960. Although used mainly for freight trip workings, the J11s were fitted with vacuum brake gear and classed 2P3F so could be called upon to work passenger trains when required, as they often were.
Robert Anderson

VETERANS ON STAVELEY 1

TOP: The bulky ex-Great Central Class L3 No. 69064, the unusual powerful design of a 2-6-4T with inside cylinders and a tractive effort of 28,760lbs, is seen on Staveley Central shed on Sunday 9th December 1951. Introduced in 1914 the class was extinct by the mid-1950s. No. 69064 is wearing a 34E Neasden shedplate. In the right background are the shearlegs, another standard feature of GC motive power depots. *Neville Stead collection/Transport Library*

BELOW: Ex-Great Northern 4-4-0 LNER Class D3 No. 2133 which had been withdrawn by 1950. Introduced in 1896 these engines were rebuilt from 1912 with larger boilers. *K.C.H. Fairey/Colour-Rail*

VETERANS ON STAVELEY 11

TOP: Not all the "Large Director" 4-4-0s were in store at Easter 1959. Here, bearing a 41H shedplate, Darnall's 62663 *Prince Albert* is in steam and ready for action by the coaling stage on Monday 30th March. Manpower shortages meant that ever younger locomen were being recruited at this time!

CENTRE: A number of ex-Great Eastern Railway tank engines gravitated to the GC for shunting duties. Seen alongside Staveley's northlight-roof shed in the 1950s is No. 68383, the last surviving J66 0-6-0 in capital stock, a class dating from 1886. Three other survivors were in departmental service at Stratford Works.
Both Neville Stead collection./ Transport Library

LEFT: The N5 0-6-2Ts were introduced by the MS&LR in 1891 and did useful work on passenger, goods and pilot duties until the end of the 1950s. No. 69263 with her 38D shedplate still looks in fine fettle as she simmers on Staveley shed. The N5s were classified 2MT by BR.
Peter Cookson

ABOVE: An evening coal train for Annesley sets out from Staveley headed by ex-ROD O4/3 2-8-0 No. 63845 on Friday 6th September 1957. *Peter Hay/Transport Library*

BELOW: By the 1960s Staveley Central was allocated a sizeable collection of the O1 2-8-0s rebuilt from the Class 04s. No. 63868 passes the engine shed and Staveley South Junction signal box with a brake van in tow. *Tom Greaves*

LEFT: Staveley Works station (previously Staveley Works for Barrow Hill) Down platform and buildings looking towards Chesterfield on 2nd March 1963. There was a goods yard on the right with a 1 1/2 ton crane but equipped to handle only general goods. In company days it was shared with the London & North Western Railway and then the LMS. *Chris Gammell/Photos from the Fifties*

BELOW: An O4 2-8-0 disturbs the tranquil waters of the Chesterfield Canal as it rumbles a train of empty iron ore tipplers through Staveley Works station at 5.25pm on Saturday 28th April 1962. *Robert Anderson*

Having passed Staveley South Junction signal box in the fork with the main line, our Chesterfield branch train curves away right and enters a cutting, passing under bridges carrying Inkersall Road and then Chesterfield Road. We then curve left onto an embankment and are joined on our right by the Chesterfield Canal and, on its opposite bank begins the vast industrial expanse of Staveley Iron and Chemical Works. Immediately after passing over Trough Brook Road we enter Staveley Works station where the canal passes underneath the platforms and onto our left side. On the left a siding goes over the canal to an opencast site, immediately behind some railway cottages. On the right are various sidings and connections into the works followed by a more extensive spread of sidings. Shortly, we curve left to come alongside the Midland "Old Road" in the Whittington area. Still with the canal on our left, we pass through Brimmington station with its goods shed, two other sidings, cattle dock and 10 ton crane, also once shared with the LNWR. Then we pass under the "Old Road" and the Midland Dore line to be joined on the right by Sheepbridge Sidings which form an interchange between the GC and Midland systems, providing the GC side with direct access to Sheepbridge Works. From the far end of the sidings the ex-Midland Canal Branch goes over the River Rother to the British Thompson Houston and Lamp Caps Ltd.(later AEI) factories with their own internal railway. A siding follows the foot of the Dore line embankment to Pearson's pottery. After passing Lockoford Siding on the left and under Lockoford Road, we curve gently right as a siding to the sewerage works comes into view on the left along with the turntable, followed by the Shell-BP Wharf Lane terminal on the right, and then Chesterfield Central goods depot on the left before coming to rest in the station.

ABOVE: On the Chesterfield Loop. D11/1 "Large Director" 4-4-0 No. 62661 *Gerard Powys Dewhurst* calls at Staveley Works station with the Saturdays Only 12.3pm Chesterfield Central-Sheffield Victoria on 12th September 1959. There was a fair gathering of enthusiasts here on what it was feared would be the last days in service for these iconic Great Central engines. At the end of this summer timetable the few survivors would go back in to store, but they would have one more season helping with heavy summer traffic in 1960 before the scrapman beckoned. Fortunately, No. 62660 *Butler Henderson* is preserved in the National Collection and at the time of writing was back in Staveley, as a resident of Barrow Hill roundhouse. *John Beaumont/Robert Anderson Collection*

BELOW: O4/7 2-8-0 No. 63661(a reboilered version introduced in 1939) simmers alone alongside Staveley Works signal box at 5.5pm on Saturday 28th April 1962, its crew quite possibly enjoying a teatime brew with the signalman. Modellers especially notice the sheet draped between the cab roof and the tender to provide shelter from the elements when working tender first. The station goods yard was situated behind the signal box but it had closed on 1st December 1955. *Robert Anderson*

ABOVE: At Chesterfield Central, Darnall B1 4-6-0 No. 61312 is arriving with a 1950s class A service, possibly a Manchester Central-Leicester semi-fast. An N5 0-6-2T stands on pilot duty. Behind 61312 and its train is the goods depot. In 1956 it was listed by the Handbook of Stations as having a 10-ton permanent crane and able to handle all classes of goods except livestock. While the station closed to passengers on 4th March 1963, goods facilities survived until 11th September 1967 with private sidings thereafter, thus ensuring a GC presence in Chesterfield for a little longer. *Neville Stead collection/Transport Library*

BELOW: The magnificent sight of two "Large Directors" side by side at Chesterfield Central. No. 62667 *Somme* in the bay platform with a local service(possibly the 4.20pm all stations) to Sheffield while No. 62666 *Zeebrugge* waits in the centre to work a later service, possibly the 5.9pm all stations to Sheffield. Unfortunately, the date is not recorded. The factory in the left background was served by a private siding extending from the goods yard *Neville Stead collection/Transport Library*

OPPOSITE PAGE TOP: B1 4-6-0 No. 61047 is beset by a seriously leaking steam collector while rolling alongside Chesterfield Central's timber Up side buildings when arriving with the 12.41pm Sheffield Victoria-Nottingham Victoria on Saturday 17th December 1960.
Leslie R. Freeman/Transport Treasury

RIGHT: The modest timber station entrance at Chesterfield Central hardly conveyed the impression that important services departed from the platforms below and indeed the station was served in the most by only local trains. Even so, some effort was made at ornamentation on the crown of the hipped roof over the booking hall. The platform buildings can just be seen down below on the right.
David Lawrence/Photos from the Fifties

CHESTERFIELD CENTRAL SATURDAY PASSENGER SERVICES SUMMER 1961

am

12.8	11.35pmFO Sheffield-Hastings *1st July-25th August*
7.1	6.3 Sheffield-Nottingham all stations
7.2	6.0 Nottingham-Manchester Piccadilly
7.36	To Skegness *1st July-26th August*
8.17	To Blackpool North *1st July-2nd September*
8.47arr	8.0 All stations from Sheffield
9.9	7.30 Leicester-Sheffield *Non-stop to Sheffield*
9.24	All stations to Sheffield
9.40	9.5 Sheffield-Bournemouth Central
11.13	10.24 Sheffield-Nottingham all stations

pm

12.0	All stations to Sheffield
1.33	12.46 Sheffield-Nottingham all stations
2.0arr	9.40am from Blackpool *8th July-2nd September*
2.42	1.55 Sheffield-Leicester all stations
3.1arr	1.0 all stations from Leicester
4.20	All stations to Sheffield
4.49arr	1.47 from Skegness *1st July-26th August*
5.9	All stations to Sheffield
5.10	4.20 Sheffield-Nottingham all stations
5.35	10.14 Hastings-Sheffield *15th July-26th August*
5.53	11.0 Bournemouth Central-Sheffield
6.34	5.49 Sheffield-Leicester
6.53	5.56 Nottingham-Sheffield all stations
7.53	6.55 Nottingham-Sheffield
9.34	8.50 Sheffield-Nottingham
10.11arr	9.20 from Nottingham
10.26FO	9.55 Sheffield-Portsmouth Harbour
10.34	All stations except Darnall to Sheffield

ABOVE: The next station going south after Chesterfield was Grassmoor where there were branches to Bond's Main and Grassmoor collieries. This view shows the station signal box looking towards Chesterfield and what remains of the station which closed to both passengers and goods on 28th October 1940 but was still listed in 1956 as available for wagonload coal and mineral traffic. There was also East Street Siding. *Railway Station Photographs*

BELOW: The Chesterfield Loop rejoined the main line at Heath. This is the station looking north on Saturday 8th October 1966, just over a month after the main line's closure. Beyond the bridge on the left was the goods yard with warehouse, cattle dock and 1½-ton crane but closed on 12th June 1965, and on the right the branch to Williamthorpe Colliery which curved round and underneath the GC main line into the colliery yard. Coming south through the right hand bridge span and behind the station was a branch to Holmewood Colliery. The signals are "off" but there will be no trains. *Mike Mitchell/Transport Treasury*

ABOVE: The closed Great Central main line looking north on Saturday 8th October 1966 towards Heath where the station is in the very far distance. On the right is Holmewood (formerly Hardwick) Colliery with Holmewood Colliery signal box on the left. The Midland branch from the Hasland-Pilsley loop comes into the colliery from the left, passing underneath the main line(see page 40,) the underbridge superstructure just visible in the middle distance. *Mike Mitchell /Transport Treasury*

BELOW: Pilsley station looking north, closed to passengers and goods with effect from 2nd November 1959 and now descending into dereliction. On the right is the branch to Pilsley Colliery from sidings south of the station. The branch rises up and curves over the main line to reach the colliery, the structures of which are just visible through the mist. Immediately left of the station but not visible, is the Midland Pilsley-Hasland loop. *Railway Station Photographs*

ABOVE: Looking south at Pilsley station, closed and boarded up. On the left are connections leading to the exchange sidings for Pilsley Colliery from where a branch to the colliery passed through the bridge span on the left. *Railway Station Photographs*

BELOW: South of Pilsley came Tibshelf Town, seen here with Staveley's 01 2-8-0 No. 63868 heading a Staveley-Annesley Through Freight on Friday 12th March 1965. Tibshelf Town closed to passengers when stopping services were withdrawn on 4th March 1963 and to goods on 4th May 1964. *Neville Stead collection/Transport Library*

ABOVE: A part of the Great Central since being absorbed in 1907, the Lancashire, Derbyshire & East Coast Railway had its western terminus at Chesterfield Market Place station, though to be a terminus wasn't the plan. This 1930s view of Market Place station, still in its heyday, shows Ex-GC 4-4-2T LNER No. 6129 awaiting departure with a set of six-wheeled coaches. A varied selection of bogie coaches are in the platform on the left, including some Great Central vehicles with a distinct continental look.
Railway Station Photographs

Chesterfield Market Place was listed in the 1938 Railway Clearing House Handbook of Stations as equipped to handle all classes of goods with a 10-ton permanent crane. There was a connection to Chesterfield Tube Co. and Bryan, Donkin & Co. works besides that on the Brampton branch.

It closed to passengers with effect from 3rd December 1951 and to goods with effect from 4th March 1957.

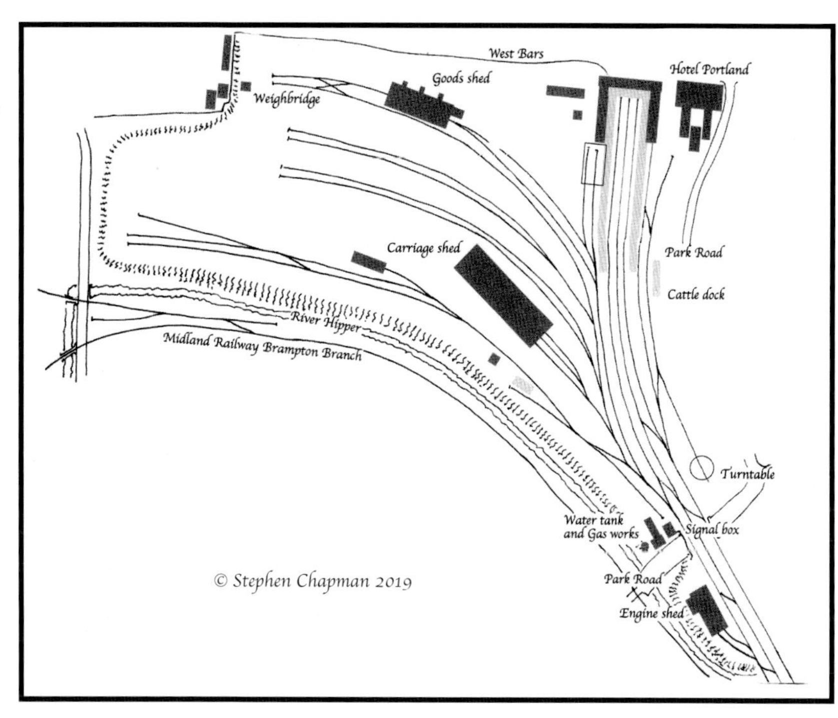

RIGHT: The layout at Chesterfield Market Place c1900. *Not to scale*
By 1918 the engine shed had completely gone and the carriage shed reduced to one road while the set of sidings immediately above the river Hipper had been shortened and the bulge of land on the left let to an industrial concern. By the 1930s the pair of sidings immediately above the carriage shed had been reduced to one and a loading dock provided.

Chesterfield Market Place weekday passenger service Summer 1946

am		pm	
7.34arr	7.0 from Shirebrook North	1.15	All stations to Mansfield
7.50	To Arkwright Town, Bolsover, Scarcliffe, Shirebrook North, Warsop,Edwinstowe, Ollerton, Boughton, Tuxford Central, Fledborough, Clifton-on-Trent, Doddington & Harby, Skellingthorpe, Lincoln.	2.26	12.45 from Lincoln
		4.0	All stations as above to Lincoln
		4.56	4.0 from Mansfield
		5.18so	2.20 from Skegness *8th June-28th September*
8.5so	To Bolsover, Shirebrook North, Warsop, Lincoln, Skegness. *8th June-28th September*	6.15	All stations to Shirebrook North
8.56arr	8.27 from Shirebrook North	8.3	6.25 from Lincoln
9.40	All stations as above to Lincoln	9.0	Bolsover, Shirebrook North
11.15arr	9.35 from Lincoln		

No Sunday service

ABOVE: J11 0-6-0 No. 64321 of Langwith Junction shed is the engine awaiting departure from Chesterfield Market Place on Saturday 24th June 1950, the year before withdrawal of passenger services following the serious problems with Bolsover Tunnel. The goods yard is on the left.

LEFT: Chesterfield Market Place signal box with the typically GC monolithic water tower behind it.
Both Neville Stead collection/ Transport Library

RIGHT: Rather lavish station buildings and grand entrance to a great terminus but, yes, this is Chesterfield Market Place. A wonderful example of ambition exceeding harsh reality. The board beneath the clock proclaims "The Dukeries Route. Lancashire, Derbyshire & East Coast Company." The posters behind the boys advertise excursions to Lincoln, Skegness and Cleethorpes.
Ray Woodmore Colln.

ABOVE: In 1948 an exhibition was staged in Market Place goods yard to mark the centenary of George Stephenson's death and, no doubt, to promote the newly nationalised railway with immaculate engines bearing British Railways on their tenders. Leading this line-up is B1 4-6-0 No. 61085. In 1961, as a Leicester Central engine, it would be the first of the class to be withdrawn in the normal course of events - just one other had already been written off in a collision. Behind it is D10 "Small Director" No. 62658 *Prince George* visiting from Trafford Park. Beyond it are representatives of the Midland side. Behind the B1 are the station buildings which were also the LD&EC's headquarters, thus explaining their ornate and extensive construction. *Neville Stead Collection/Transport Library*

BELOW: One of the Midland representatives gives the 1940s public an impression of how things used to be on the Midland side in the days of the old company. It is the recently preserved Johnson 2-4-0 No. 158A. *Tom Greaves*

ABOVE: Another Midland representative, preserved 4-2-2 No. 118. Behind it is an example of contemporary intermodal freight transport with a Co-op road milk tanker on a rail wagon. *Tom Greaves*

BELOW: Modernity at that time - newly rebuilt ex-LMS Patriot 4-6-0 No. 45529, only just named *Stephenson* - appropriate since George Stephenson had made Chesterfield his home. *Tom Greaves.*

RIGHT: Two miles along the line came Duckmanton Tunnel, disused since the end of goods traffic in 1957. Just what was going on here on 26th April 1973 is not recorded. The skeletal structure is clearly designed to match the tunnel profile and is topped with a working platform to facilitate repairs before blocking the entrance with backfill. Above the tunnel are signs of a landslip. The headshunt for lines into Arkwright Colliery terminated at this spot but had been shortened by this time. *Robert Anderson archive*

BELOW: After Duckmanton Tunnel came Arkwright Colliery and then Arkwright Town station, still complete but overgrown when visited by this DMU railtour in June 1961. The station was to have been called Duckmanton but was in the event named after the estate of Sir Richard Arkwright through which the line passed. *Railway Station Photographs*

ABOVE: The bare platforms of Arkwright Town looking east from Sutton Lane on Saturday 8th October 1966. A line of wagons can be seen at Arkwright Town Junction in the far distance. Beyond the wagons is the end of the line near the former Markham Junction. The erstwhile goods yard on the right was listed in the 1956 Handbook of Stations as being being equipped to handle general goods, furniture vans, carriages, motor cars, portable engines and machines on wheels, but it had no permanent crane. The 1938 handbook listed Arkwright Town as being able to handle passengers and all classes of goods but still with no crane. Before completion of Duckmanton Junctions, a branch climbed up on the left from a point beyond the station, over a level crossing and to a sidings connection with the GC main line. *Mike Mitchell/Transport Treasury*

LEFT: Arkwright Town Junction as it was on 8th October 1966. The railway through here and the station survived until 1988 to serve Arkwright Colliery - as a 9-mile long single track from Beighton Junction with only one train allowed at a time. The track in the foreground climbs up from Duckmanton North Junction. *Mike Mitchell/ Transport Treasury*

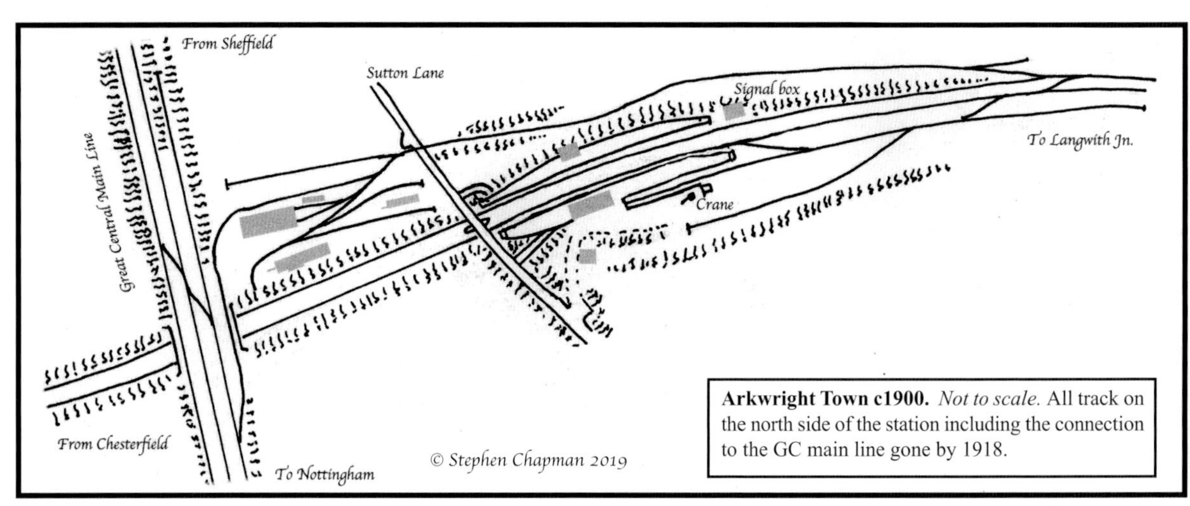

Arkwright Town c1900. *Not to scale.* All track on the north side of the station including the connection to the GC main line gone by 1918.

ABOVE: Duckmanton Junction on the GC main line looking north on Saturday 8th October 1966, a month after complete closure of the main line south of this point. In the foreground is the site of the former Duckmanton South Junction. The trackbed going left denotes the curve which climbed round to the right and crossed over the main line to East Junction, the bridge piers just visible minus the superstructure. At East Junction it joined the spur from north-facing Duckmanton North Junction to the east-facing Arkwright Town Junction. Another curve connected East Junction to the main line in a south-facing direction, the trackbed of which is visible on the right. *Mike Mitchell/Transport Treasury*

BELOW: After Bolsover Tunnel the LD&EC came to Bolsover South station, pictured here as it was in its prime, shortly after the GC takeover. The 1938 Handbook of Stations listed Bolsover South(just Bolsover until 1950) as having a 3-ton crane and being equipped to handle all classes of goods - in fact much better equipped than its Midland neighbour but it closed to all traffic with effect from 3rd December 1951. The Bolsover Home Grown Fruit Preserving Co. was listed as having a siding here. *Railway Station Photographs*

ABOVE: After Bolsover came Scarcliffe. This old postcard view of the island platform station looking east also shows the goods yard on the left with loading dock and cattle pens and, beyond the station in the middle distance, the signal box. The 1938 Handbook of stations listed Scarcliffe as able to deal with all classes of goods but with no permanent crane. *Railway Station Photographs*

THE ASHOVER LIGHT RAILWAY

BELOW: Much has been written about this notable narrow gauge line from Clay Cross and in such expert detail that it is not intended to repeat it here. However, the following half dozen pictures are provided for the sake of completeness. It was of course well known for its Baldwin 4-6-0 tank engines released from military service at the end of the First World War. Seen here at Butts with a Stephenson Locomotive Society special composed of open wagons in August 1947 is *Joan*. *Graham Ellis/Transport Treasury*

ABOVE: Although once providing a passenger service the Ashover Light Railway was really an industrial line, intended for bringing limestone from quarries at Fallgate to the Clay Cross company's furnaces. This is the Ashover yard at Clay Cross with standard gauge wagons on the slightly higher ground. The huge iron works slag tip is on the left. *Railway Station Photographs*

RIGHT: The engine shed at Clay Cross with *Joan* in residence and unusual coaling stage on the right. *T.G.Wassell/Photos from the Fifties*

LEFT: The Ashover passenger station at Clay Cross some time after withdrawal of passenger services. The building is boarded up and the track appears to have been lifted at this spot. Worthy of note is the incline on the slag tip. *T.G. Wassell/Photos from the Fifties*

ABOVE: *Joan* taking water at Fallgate Quarry during the SLS tour of August 1947. *Graham Ellis/Transport Treasury*

BELOW: The line was not entirely steam and this everyday view from the late 1940s shows a 4-wheel petrol loco with a train of limestone for Clay Cross. Judging by the armoured look, it is also ex-War Department. *Sydney Roberts/Transport Treasury*

ON INDUSTRIAL LINES

The many industrial complexes and collieries around Chesterfield once employed large numbers of industrial shunting locomotives, steam and diesel, on their own, often extensive and complex railway systems. Apart from illustrating a selection of these the engines, the following pictures allow us a rare glimpse inside the long lost industrial plants that were once so vital to the Chesterfield area economy. TOP: The NCB's Coal Products division employed a fleet of seven diesel shunting locomotives at its Avenue coke and by-products plant, Wingerworth. The pair seen on Monday 17th October 1977 are Hudswell, Clarke 0-6-0 D1388 of 1970(left) and Hunslet 0-6-0 No. 4511 of 1955 - similar to the BR Class 05 and one of five built specially for the new plant at the time of its opening. *Adrian Booth*

RIGHT: Apart from the Ashover Light Railway, Clay Cross foundry had internal railways of four different gauges - 3ft, metre, 2ft and standard. On Saturday 17th June 1978 this Lister diesel was seen moving iron pipes at the spun pipe works which employed the 2ft gauge system with six locomotives. Clay Cross foundry also had two 1954-built standard gauge Ruston & Hornsby diesels, *Jane* and *Caroline,* but standard gauge working ceased in 1978.
Adrian Booth

RIGHT: Situated near the long closed Clay Cross No.4 Colliery and the Springfield Brick and Tile works, and immediately east of the North Midland main line near the site of Clay Cross station, was this coal mining survivor. The cable-hauled tubs on the 2ft gauge tramway leading into the "small mine" at Strathfield Colliery are seen still very active on Tuesday 7th May 1985. The mine lasted until 1988 when it became worked out. This tramway was typical of those used at small mines around the area, the last one, at Eckington, surviving in use until 2019.

BELOW: The Campbell Brickworks next to Barrow Hill engine shed employed a 2ft gauge railway for bringing clay from the claypit to the works. One of the two locos, Motorail 4-wheel diesel mechanical 60s364, built 1948, is seen with a pair of skips on Tuesday 6th November 1973.
Both Adrian Booth

LEFT: In common with many such installations, the Yorkshire Water Authority's sewerage works at Whittington had its internal narrow gauge system and this is where one of its four 2ft gauge Ruston & Hornsby 4-wheel diesels is seen on Tuesday 13th March 1979. The railway was out of use by 1980. *Adrian Booth*

RIGHT: Out of use deep within Staveley Works on 6th October 1962 were these beautifully lined out 0-4-0STs built by William Bagnall & Co of Stafford. At the front is Bagnall No. 12(builder's No. 2822) and behind it Bagnall No.11(builder's No. 2821.)
Robert Anderson

BELOW: Just why Brush-Beyer Peacock 0-4-0 diesel electric No.88 (Brush 334/BP7941 of 1960) should be shunting in Summit Sidings is a bit of a mystery. This series of engines was destined for Renishaw and Rotherham Park Gate Works, and since it looks brand new it must have been waylaid at Staveley for some reason while on its way there.
Tom Greaves

ABOVE: Despite the presence of heavy engineering, Chesterfield would not automatically be thought of as a centre of locomotive building but Markham & Co.built a grand total of 19 engines, mostly for use in the local area. This one out of use at Staveley Iron Works on Saturday 28th April 1962 is *Duston,* built at Markham's Broad Oaks works in 1909, builder's No. 103, rebuilt 1924. Markham began their works numbering series at 101, possibly to give the impression that they were long standing and experienced locomotive builders. *Robert Anderson*

BELOW: This Chesterfield-built Markham 0-4-0ST *Gladys*, builders No. 109 of 1894, is pictured in store at Staveley Works on 21st March 1969. *Adrian Booth.* **See Railway Memories No.27 for another Markham loco in George Slater & Co.'s yard at Beighton. *Gladys* is preserved at the Midland Railway Trust, Butterley.**

ABOVE: Renishaw Iron Works operated a fleet of locomotives on its internal railway. Alongside the blast furnaces on Sunday 5th March 1961 is Hudswell, Clarke 0-6-0ST *Renishaw Ironwo*rks *No.6,* builder's No. 1366 of 1919 and now preserved at the Tanfield Railway Co. Durham. In the 19th Century the Renishaw Works had an internal railway called The Cottam Railway which brought coal and iron from small mines within its own precincts. *R.C. Riley/Transport Treasury*

BELOW: In the engine shed sidings at Renishaw Iron Works on 5th March 1961 was 0-4-0ST No.3. Parts of another saddle tank can be seen behind it while BR wagons are in higher level sidings beyond the lagoon. *R.C. Riley/Transport Treasury*

Awaiting their destiny in the scrapyard of Steel Breaking & Dismantling near Tapton Junction on Sunday 5th March 1961 was this trio of antiquated saddle tanks. TOP: This 0-4-0 is *Lily,* built by Markham & Co. in 1909.

CENTRE: This 0-4-0 *Peterstone* has ancient unidentified origins but its works plate says it was rebuilt by Manning Wardle of Leeds in 1907.

BOTTOM: The short-wheelbase of 0-6-0 *Isaac Limb* gives it a cartoon-like appearance. Unfortunately it has no worksplate to identify it but there are signs of a once attractive lined livery.
All R.C. Riley/Transport Treasury

NCB EAST MIDLANDS DIVISION NO.1 (CHESTERFIELD) AREA 1956

Arkwright Colliery
Avenue Coking Plant
Bolsover Colliery
Bond's Main Colliery
Clay Cross Washery, coke ovens and by-products plant.
Creswell Colliery
Danesmoor(Parkhouse) Colliery, Clay Cross
Glapwell Colliery
Grassmoor Colliery, coke ovens & by-products plant
Hardwick coke ovens & by- products plant
Hartington Siding
Holmewood Colliery
Ireland Colliery
Langwith Colliery
Markham Colliery
Morton Colliery
Oxcroft Colliery
Pilsley Colliery
Ramcroft Colliery
Renishaw Park Colliery
Westthorpe Colliery
Whitwell Colliery
Williamthorpe Colliery

TOP: A lovely picture in unlovely yet fascinating surroundings, Peckett 0-4-0ST No.2(builders No. 1921 of 1936) shunts at Bolsover Coalite & Chemical plant on 8th March 1964. Despite their surroundings, Bolsover engines were smartly turned out in green and red livery. The Coalite Works soldiered on after the neighbouring colliery had closed and in 1993 was receiving coal from Bevercotes Colliery, Nottinghamshire, in 2-3 trainloads a week.

CENTRE: At the Bolsover Colliery on the same day was Avonside 0-4-0ST *David* (builders No. 1999 of 1927.) Bolsover Colliery went over to MGR operation in 1989 and locomotives were no longer required - but that was long long after these beautiful engines had disappeared. It closed in 1993.

BOTTOM: A shed scene at Oxcroft Colliery on 8th March 1964 with Hawthorn, Leslie 0-4-0ST *Bolsover No.1* (No. 3631 of 1925.) Behind it is Hunslet 0-4-0ST 3289 of 1945
All Alec Swain/ Transport Treasury

ABOVE: Pictured at Ramcroft Colliery on Friday 8th March 1964 is *Ramcroft No.12*, built by Avonside of Bristol in 1916, works No. 1727. *Alec Swain/Transport Treasury*

BELOW: At Renishaw Park Colliery on Wednesday 2nd June 1982, 1967-built Hudswell, Clarke 0-4-0 diesel 1387 pushes empty MGR wagons up to the pit from the exchange sidings with the "Old Road" which is in the foreground. *Adrian Booth*